Journey From Drugs to Jesus

The Testimony of

Tom Jackson

Published by:

IN HIS STEPS PUBLISHING
6500 Clito Road
Statesboro, Georgia 30461 (U.S.A.)
1-912-587-4400

© 2010 by Tom Jackson
ALL RIGHTS RESERVED!

Cover Photo by ISTOCKPHOTO.COM. Permission granted for use.

ISBN: 978-1-58535-204-3 (13)
ISBN: 1-58535-204-7 (10)

Dedication

This book is dedicated to my Lord and Savior, Jesus Christ, for making a way for me where there was no way; to God the Father for sending His Only Son to pay that price for me, and to God, the Holy Spirit, who guided my words for this book and performed all of the miraculous things that have happened in my life to produce a testimony for His glory. Without the leading of the Holy Spirit, this book and my life would not have been possible. Thank You, Lord, for all You have done and are doing in my life.

To my wife, Dell, who has stuck with me through thick-and-thin. I love you and thank you for all of your prayers for me. You are the best! I have more love for you now than ever before.

To my son, Kaiser, whose relationship with me teaches me more and more about how I am to come to my heavenly Father. You never cared if I was writing or praying or anything else. You knew you were always welcome and allowed to bust right on in the door and come to ask me anything. I love you and thank God for you. You are an awesome son!

To my mom and dad, who never gave up on me. And even when there were doubts and questions in your minds if I would live or die or be able to have a normal life, you never once let on to me that I couldn't do anything anybody else could do, and inspired me to live my life. And when I was totally crazy, you kept loving me through it all. Thank you so much! I love you both more now than ever.

Contents

Chapter One
Born Very Different 7
Chapter Two
Introduction to Drugs, As If I Needed Another
Obstacle 15
Chapter Three
Drugs, Drugs and More Drugs! 18
Chapter Four
Body Wearing Down, But Still in Bondage 25
Chapter Five
My Real Encounter With Jesus 28
Chapter Six
Surprise! You Still Have to Reap What You Sow! 32
Chapter Seven
More Grace and the Baptism of the Holy Spirit! 35
Chapter Eight
The Call of God: Stepping Into God's Plan for
My Life 48
Chapter Nine
My Heart for Worship 57
Chapter Ten
Breaking Out of Religion Into Relationship 66
Chapter Eleven
New Direction for the Call: A Call to the Hot House 82
Chapter Twelve
Testimonies of the Miraculous 91
Chapter Thirteen
Staying Strong Through Death 116
Chapter Fourteen
Do Not Neglect Salvation 126

Chapter 1

Born Very Different

My mom and dad had been married for several years and already had my oldest brother, Scott. They had also had my other brother, Michael-Paul, who was born with spina bifida. He was alive the full term, but when he was born he had a large hole in his back and died at birth. This was very traumatic to my parents, to say the least. With the very sad outcome with Michael-Paul, my parents and their doctor wanted to take extra precautions with the next pregnancy, which was to be me. Now keep in mind that in 1977 they did not have sonograms, so they never knew what the child would be until the actual birth. But since my brother had spina bifida they wanted to do a check on my mom to see whether or not I might have had the same problem. This test showed them I did not have spina bifida, and it also let them in on the secret that most others at this time didn't know they were having another boy.

With the cat out of the bag, now they could begin to plan for my birth and come up with my name. They named me after both of my granddads and chose the name, Thomas Wilson Jackson. Thomas was my mom's dad; Wilson was my father's dad. So I was named and they chose to call me Tom.

Now everyone in our small Macon, Georgia community heard the news and whenever my mom came around, everyone made sure to say hello to me. Now this is a common thing today, but back then, this was very different and I think it was very significant for me to become the person I am today.

So my mom was eating very healthy and was doing a lot of walking to try to ensure a healthy baby and good pregnancy.

So early on the morning of April 20, 1978, my mom awoke at around 4:00AM. She was having pains and so she woke my dad up. She wasn't sure if it was time to have me yet though. My dad had a business presentation he was supposed to present in Atlanta that same morning. So my mom reassured him she was going to be all right. And he went on to Atlanta to make the presentation.

Shortly after he left, my mom went into contractions. She was trying to get the last load of clothes washed and get her hair and makeup ready for the day. But I was ready to come out, and I messed up all her plans for that day.

Her contractions were getting closer and closer together. She and my four-year old brother were kneeling down and counting the minutes between the contractions. When they were five minutes apart my mom called my grandparents to come and get her and take her to the hospital. My dad was from Macon so they lived about four blocks away from his parents. We called them Grandma and Papa. They quickly came over and picked my mom and Scott up. They rushed us by the local daycare, which was a neighborhood friend. They dropped Scott off as fast as they could and then got right on the interstate. The interstate was literally across the street from the daycare and the hospital was only about 4 exits down from where we lived. As they drove down the road, you have to keep in mind this was the time that CB radios were at their peak of popularity. So my Papa had his CB and he was on it letting everyone know he had a pregnant woman who was in labor. Just picture this, a huge burgundy Cadillac coming down the interstate with a pregnant woman in labor and a grandpa on the CB saying, "Clear the Highway, we are coming down I-75. Clear the Highway, we got a pregnant woman about to give birth." My grandma was up front holding my mom's hand in the back seat with pillows and sheets. They were ready for me to be born in the car if necessary.

Meanwhile, my dad was on his way to Atlanta. Now keep in mind that there were no cell phones or car phones, so there was literally no way to notify dad, until he reached his destination, that it was time for me to be born. So when he finally did arrive, they immediately told him he had to get back to Macon right away because my mom had gone into labor. When he left he was in a work van that was supposed to get loaded with equipment. So when they said he needed to leave immediately, he was not able to leave in the van, he needed a ride. But God was looking out for him that day. A woman there said she could get him a police escort if he had a car, but he told her he didn't. She told him just to wait right there. Very soon a Georgia State Patrol pulled up. My dad got in and said that the Trooper had a bag of "Red Man" chewing tobacco and a mouth full of it. He had a coffee can too that he was using to spit in. He turned to my dad and said, "How fast do you want to go."

My dad said, "Well it's not life or death, but I want to get there." So that Trooper took him as far as he could and then met up with another Trooper, and he got in with him. He rode with about four different Troopers to get to Macon, and they soon got him to the hospital.

My grandma and Papa had pulled up at the hospital and two nurses met them at the emergency room of the Coliseum Park Hospital in downtown Macon, Georgia. They quickly rushed mom to a holding room next door to the delivery room. Upon arrival, my mom was already dilated nine centimeters. Within fifteen minutes her water had broken and she was going into labor. The doctor made it just in time, and they immediately put his gloves on him. As quick as the doctor got his gloves on and sat down, I came out!

Within twenty to thirty minutes my dad arrived. He and my mom had been taking a natural child birth class. She had me with no pain medication at all. So when he came in to the hospital, he was prepared to help her. He came in wide open and he had both of his hands in the air like he was a doctor, waiting to get his gloves on for delivery, and he was yelling, "I'm trained, I'm trained!"

And the nurse said to him, "You're late, you're late!" I was already cleaned and wrapped up in my mama's arms.

But I was born very different. I was born with a massive birthmark that almost entirely surrounded my left leg and even comes up to my lower back. Along with the discoloration came a large amount of extra blood vessels, and many were oversized. They also did not have many functioning valves so the blood was able to flow backwards, depending on the positioning of my leg, whether elevated or not. Also as if that wasn't enough, my lymphatic system had problems with circulation and the fluid pools in my ankle and lower leg. That caused severe swelling. My pelvis was also tilted and twisted, so my left leg was about an inch-and-a-half shorter than my right leg. Throw in scoliosis and you have my debut on this earth, HALLELUJAH!

Now all these symptoms put together have been deemed K.T. Webber syndrome. This is a known disease now, but in 1978 it was not, and there was no treatment for it then, and very minimal things can be done to help it now. Back then, as you could imagine, my parents were very concerned. This concern drove them into prayer and seeking answers from God. They put me on prayer chains all over the Nation and all over the world. There is really no telling how many people have actually prayed for me before I even really started out my life.

My mom and dad were Christians but had grown up in denominations that were very traditional and religious. There was no doubt they had Jesus as their Savior, but they did not know Him as Healer, Deliverer, Dead Raiser, or Miracle Worker. But this situation drove them on a quest for the truth about Jesus. The standard religious answers were not cutting it. You know the ones: *God does everything for a reason*; *it must be God's will.* First of all these are not scriptures, and secondly, they are truly a religious cop-out for someone who doesn't have a clue why something has happened, so instead of being humble and admitting they don't know why it happened, they keep their pride and give you some religious answer that they too have heard others pawn off on people who have devastating circumstances.

Well my mom, being a mom, was having a very hard time dealing with this, which is totally understandable. If you have children then you understand. So her quest had started for the truth about the REAL JESUS. She began to search the scriptures and began to see that Jesus was not only a healer on the side, but that this was something He did everywhere He went. She began to see something very different in the Word of God than what she had heard all of her life. She saw that there was actually a Baptism with God's Holy Spirit, and that there was power and miracles at hand. So she began to seek the LORD like never before. And the end result was a beautiful thing.

My mom told me of the day she actually received the Baptism of the Holy Spirit, and when she did, there was evidence of Speaking in Tongues.

She said when we lived in Macon, she stayed home and kept my older brother, Scott, and me. So she would usually get up early before us and before my dad left for work and go for a walk in our small neighborhood. She said that one day as she was walking, she began to pray for her family. She remembers specifically praying that day for her brother. Then as she was praying, the Holy Spirit overshadowed her and manifested Himself to her, and actually touched her tongue. Then she began to pray in a heavenly language she had never spoken before. She felt as though God had control of her tongue and would not let go. This is hilarious to me to think about my mom walking around the neighborhood praying in tongues and having no control, and just being amazed, and probably looking amazed too. I wish I could have been there!

(*Shundala! Shundala! Shaca ma boo boo!*) I laugh, but I know it is real.

So now she had actually had an amazing encounter with God that changed her life forever. She knew there was more, and she had just experienced a small taste of it. So she and my dad kept on pursuing God until he too had a similar encounter.

It was like pulling nails to get my dad to share his testimony with me, and he is not shy or short of words, he was just messing with me for some reason on this particular day. But I asked him if he had ever been baptized with the Holy Spirit and he said yes, then he was very quiet. I said, "Where were you at?"

He said, "In Mount Paran Church of God."

I said, "How do you know you were baptized with the Holy Spirit?"

He said, "I spoke in tongues." And I rejoiced that I actually had both of my parents receive this baptism.

All of this comes into play in my life later on, and I actually had no idea of this until way later on in my life.

As you can imagine, growing up with one leg that is totally different from the other, was very tough. It limited me some, but my parents were very smart about raising me, and I didn't feel like I missed anything growing up. I didn't play sports for school or any recreation teams. Instead, I caught all kinds of animals and played with them, and loved the woods. And my dad was always picking up turtles and snakes and bringing them home for me.

I did often have problems with my leg: such as blood clots and pains from the swelling. Over the years I had to try many different kinds of support stockings to try to keep the leg from swelling and causing me pain and discomfort.

There were also times of ridicule and being picked on because of my leg. I went through times of confusion and low-self esteem. I was insecure at times, and I really had to deal with a lot to go to the beach or get around people who weren't my family members in shorts. I experienced so many times where I would cry out to God in fits of "Why me, why do I have to have a leg like this?" It was very difficult but I always tried to do as much as I could and make the most of everything I could.

Along with the leg problems came several operations, some operations to remove blood clots and other procedures over the years. So I was well acquainted with pain and tough situations at a very early age. Actually, the first surgery I ever had was when I was only four-years old and had to have a tumor removed from my waistline that was as big as a grown man's hand. I still have the scar. I have a memory of this operation and it is about the oldest memory I have. I can remember being so small and having all these nurses and doctors around me on one of those hospital beds. When they tried to put that gas mask on me, I can remember going ballistic on them and I actually was kicking nurses and trying to punch them, and at four-years old, they had to each grab my arms and legs and physically restrain me and hold me down to put the mask on my mouth to administer the anesthesia. I think this was very traumatic, and I can still remember the fight. I was a tough little sucker. But they got me and this was my first surgery. This impacted me so much so that when I had to have other operations or procedures as a young child, I would ask them to stick me and administer the anesthesia intravenously. When most kids are scared of getting stuck, I was asking for it because the mask was torture to me. I would literally ask as a small child for them to give it to me in my vein. I did not want to have to go through the fight or the taste of that stinking gas ever again.

As I am writing this and kind of having to relive it, it is very emotional, but I know where the story goes, not ends, but where it is going, and the end will have to be written with time to come.

There were many times I can remember crying myself to sleep wondering why I had to have a leg different from everyone else. This was really so tough mentally as well as physically, to go through as a child. I am very grateful for having such loving parents, as well as grandparents. They all spoiled me as best they could. But in all sincerity, they were never sure how long I might live. They never once even so much as hinted around to that, but I know that to be true now.

Chapter Two

Introduction to Drugs,
As if I Needed Another Obstacle!

Now as I grew up, I had become a very comical young fellow. I wanted to fit in so badly that I did all kinds of crazy things, and was known as one of the crazy guys in school. I did whatever and said whatever to get people to like me. So I was an accident waiting to happen.

I was born in Macon, Georgia, then we moved to Atlanta, Georgia. I was very young in the first move, so I really don't have any memory of it. We moved into a different house while living in Atlanta and I do have memory of that.

In the second house we lived in there, we stayed from the time I was in Kindergarten to second grade.

Then we made a very big move. We moved from Atlanta, to Rhine, Georgia. From Atlanta, with literally millions of people, to Rhine, with literally six hundred, and only one traffic light, this proved to be culture shock! Can you imagine coming from hundreds of traffic lights to one, and it is still this way in April, 2010! (I love it too!)

With this move came time to have to make all new friends. I had a few cousins and knew a few people already from earlier visits, but now I was coming to stay. We moved into an old, old farmhouse with no central heating and air. It had two fireplaces that were closed off. Birds lived in one and bees in the other, and that is where I learned about the birds and the bees!

Now the new school was very different. I went from a school with thousands of students, to Rhine Elementary, which had one class per grade with just a couple of hundred students—max. It was fun because it was so small. It was so small that there was actually only one teacher per grade. So all my friends were the same every year.

The county was growing and they decided to merge all the small city schools into one large school. My friends and I hated this idea because we loved our little school. This new situation meant that we would be going to school with all of our sports rivals and with kids from other towns that we didn't want to know. We were a very tight-knit community, and most of us were related somewhere down the line. So we did not like the idea of this huge change that was coming in our lives.

The day finally arrived and we were on the buses going to our new school. When this happened, I was starting the seventh grade. When I got to my class, the only person from Rhine was my teacher, which was a little relief. I only knew one boy in the whole class, and I really didn't know him that good. So I did what I did to get to know people—I acted funny and crazy. I got into trouble a lot too. But I made new friends fast, and by the second Friday I was going home with a new friend to spend the night. This was a big mistake waiting to happen.

Needless to say, at age twelve you will try anything. These are the years when young people are trying to figure out who they are and what things they like or don't like. And fear is not really a big deal to most pre-teens or teenagers. You are willing to try almost anything, even if it could kill you. Believe me I know.

So, now I am twelve-years old, going home with some guy in my class who is older because he has failed a grade somewhere down the line. But he is my friend now and we have already gotten close in the last two weeks. I talked my mom and dad into letting me go. He only lived about ten miles away so they let me go. We started out by going to the local video store and renting a movie, and getting us some potato chips. I can still remember the movie, it was terrible and we loved it. It was the *Toxic Avenger*, if you even tried to watch it now you would never be able to finish it. It is classic 80's cheese! But man, we loved it! After the movie was over, his mom and grandma had gone to bed and left us in the living room. So he went and got something and we went outside on the front porch to the swing. He pulled out a can and had some weed, (marijuana) in it. He was so young he didn't know how to roll a joint, but the joker knew how to smoke off a can, go figure. Well, without hesitation, I was in on it. He showed me how to work the can; he made a hole for the carburetor, lit the weed with his lighter, and hit it hard! So, I did the same thing. I hit it just as hard as he did. And we got high. I mean we got fried and got the munchies. I can remember we went back inside so hungry and we had already eaten all of the chips, so we started raiding the fridge and ate all the pickles. I thought it was the best thing ever and I wanted to do it again. I didn't have a clue.

So this was my introduction to weed and I liked it. I was so young though and it was hard to get a lot of it. But every chance that I had I took advantage of it and would get with my friends and smoke as often as I could, and then I started smoking cigarettes as well.

Chapter Three

Drugs, Drugs and More Drugs!

By the time I was thirteen, I bought my first car. I worked hard on farms and I was good with my money, so I saved up $500.00 and bought a two-door blue Oldsmobile Cutlass Supreme with an 8-track in it. Now I was mobile. I would drive all over Rhine. I drove to work and to church and most importantly, fishing. This, however, is not a good idea for such a young man to have so much freedom. I could buy beer in town at a local fish market. I could get cigarettes too, and sometimes we would get cigars. And every now and then some more weed.

We often camped out so we could get drunk and smoke whatever we had and not get caught. It was easy with a car in a small town with a lot of woods.

This was just the beginning for me though. As I got older my connections got better. Before long I knew where I could get weed all the time and drank every weekend.

I ended up failing the eighth grade and was getting into trouble all the time. So when I finally made it to high school, I turned sixteen in the ninth grade, and I had a truck now. This was my third vehicle and I had been trading up. Now I was in a 1959 Ford truck that was actually a hot rod with a 460 engine in it, and the body of the truck was put on a Lincoln Continental chassis. This thing would fly. There was only one other truck in town that could out run me.

While I was in the ninth grade, my mom and dad got divorced. This had a very big affect on me. I was already basically an alcoholic and drug user, but this caused me a lot of pain inside, and I didn't care even more. So all throughout high school I was drunk and high nearly every weekend, and sometimes—in school. I remember getting drunk on my left over gin on the way to school with one of my friends. We bought some Gatorade that morning and chased the gin with the Gatorade, and in those short fifteen miles to school, we were trashed. Then our class ended up walking around the school looking for leaves. It was Biology class I think. So we ended up in the parking lot with the teacher and class, and I got in my car right in front of the teacher and mixed up a big jug of gin and Gatorade and began to share it with the class. Several of us got drunk walking around the school with our teacher. No joke.

I had job and a lot of friends, and all of them got high, or drunk, or both. My county and city had, and still has, one of the highest amounts of drugs in it in the state. Drug use was and is rampant, and all too common.

I was already selling drugs in ninth grade, nothing big but getting and distributing all the same. In my high school, I can remember buying weed in homeroom from other kids. I would get a hall pass, go to the room where this one guy always had a few dime bags, and I would get one if I didn't have any that day so I could get high before I went to work at a local mechanic shop.

Lots of times I would take some guys home when we got out early for the work program at school, and we would all throw in on a bag of weed and we would smoke it all at one time. We would roll blunts and give each other shotguns, and my car would look just like *Cheech and Chong*, it would be literally smoked out and so would we. I mean, when we let the windows down, smoke would roll out of them like my car was on fire, and we would be high, out of our minds.

This was my ritual for eleventh and twelfth grade after school before I went to work. I did, however, keep a job at the same mechanic shop for over three years and I quit before I graduated, just wanting more time to party. That was a great

Idea—NOT!

Shortly after I quit my job a friend and me dropped off a friend at his job and we were about to get high and were pulled over by an undercover Drug Task Force Unit. Needless to say, they found some weed, and my friend had a malt liquor beer in his backpack. They handcuffed us together backwards as they searched my car; not the first time it had been searched and wasn't the last time.

They took me to jail and let my friend take my car to his house. My dad was out of town so I had to call my uncle to come get me out. They let me go but I would end up having to pay over $600.00 and be on probation for six months. I also lost my drivers license and had to go through DUI School, which at that time cost me another $250.00.

Although all of that happened on that Friday afternoon, I still had the party at my house which I had already planned, and I had plenty of liquor and weed and got totally trashed that night.

While I was a senior in high school, I tried cocaine for the first time. I had seen it and been around it since the eighth grade, but my friends told me the first time I ever saw any that if I had never done it to never even start, and then they proceeded to snort some in front of me. This messed me up and I remember that night that it was raining real hard and my friends wanted to go to somebody's house, so I was letting someone else drive and they were scaring the crap out of me, so when we came to a stop sign I traded places with them so that I could drive. I then slowly pulled across the street and missed the road and hit the ditch, a deep ditch! The back end of my car was sticking up in the air, kids heads hit the windshield, and school books from the back flew up front, but none of us were really hurt and the car was fine too. But I did have to call a wrecker to pull the sucker out in the rain, and it cost me fifty bucks. But the small wreck didn't stop me. Before long I was trying it again and again.

After high school I was getting drunk and high on weed

every weekend. I actually smoked weed every day of each year, even in high school, with the exception of about ten to fourteen days a year. I know because I kept up with it. It was my goal each year. Now with cocaine in the mix, I was really getting messed up. But it didn't stop there; another drug was hitting the scene called *ecstasy*. Now, as if my leg wasn't enough to deal with in my life, I had formed numerous addictions that dominated my life.

Keep in mind that all this time through school I was in a church, until I was old enough to quit going. But the religious activities had no power, and I can only remember the presence of the Lord about two or three times in my young life actually drawing me. I had also, while I was about 15 or 16, accepted Jesus and was baptized. But I had so many issues and there was no power in my church. It was just the standard issue church that certain families went there and God seldom did. I can remember my grandma and another older lady there who would pray genuine heartfelt prayers. And I can remember all the rest of us hoping they would hurry up, and wondering why they were crying while they were praying. But there were only a handful of those women like that. So, needless to say, this type of experience followed by no Power of the Holy Spirit could not overcome the power of the drugs and the addictions that came along with them.

By now my connections with drugs and drug dealers had reached a very high peak. I could get and was getting pounds of weed fronted to me. That means I didn't have to pay to get it. I could pay later because they knew I could move it; sometimes up to seven pounds at a time. Some people have gotten more but that is still a lot. We had a cocaine hook up where we could get ounces of cocaine, as many as we could afford, and as often as we wanted. We began to get in on the ecstasy; I could get hundreds of them, we called them rolls, at the time on the front too. Keep in mind they would sell for $25 to $40 a piece. Oh, yeah, and they carried a life-sentence with each pill and there was a mandatory seven years you would have to serve on each pill.

I also stumbled in on a big deal one day where I was stopping by a friend's house just to get a little weed and when he let me in, another friend was there with 1,400 hits of acid to go along with a BIG bag of powder (cocaine) and lots of high potency weed too. So I snorted a giant line with them, got a lot of weed on the front, and also cut off a little over 100 hits of the acid to boot. I didn't have to spend a dime because I had already proven myself to be able to get rid of a pile of drugs. I was well known, too well known actually. My house was known as a dope house. Living in a small town, word gets around. But so many people around me were living crooked and tons of them bought the dope from me so I never even got raided.

But when you are involved in drugs you are always paranoid. There is always fear that you will get caught looming around you, and it is not in the back of your mind, it is in the front.

One day one of my biggest fears stared me straight in the face. There was the head of the local GBI office that only lived about five or six miles away from my house. I knew who he was and he knew who I was. But one night after being high and also being very hungry, I was at the local restaurant (there is only one in Rhine), and I was very high, just standing in line. Well, the GBI agent came right up to me and I know I smelled just like weed. He told me he wanted to talk to me, so I went outside with him. Now to put this story into perspective, I am 5'7" tall on a good day, and at this time probably weighed 180 pounds when this guy is at least 6'3" and probably 230 to 240 pounds. And as if that would not be intimidating enough, I am a guilty as sin drug dealer and he is the HEAD OF THE GEORGIA BUREAU OF INVESTIGATION!

We went outside and he proceeded to tell me that they knew what we (I had a roommate at the time who was selling a lot of cocaine) were doing, and that if we didn't stop we were going down. He was nice enough to give me a chance to quit my lawbreaking and sinful ways. That should have been enough to scare me straight, but it wasn't. You see, without the Power of the Holy Spirit, the Anointing, to destroy the yoke of bondage, you cannot go free! Isaiah 10:27 states that, "It shall come to pass in that day, that his burden shall be taken away from off thy shoulder, and his yoke from off thy neck, and the yoke shall be destroyed because of the anointing."

There is no amount of religion or good advice that can break an addiction like the one that I was in bondage too; it has to be the Anointing of God! And believe it or not, I did not even think about quitting. All I was thinking about was how to look the part and to get that cocaine out of my house because that is what really draws the attention of the police. That is what I thought anyway, you know like weed was no big deal. So my friend took all of the powder out of the house and hid it in the woods and if somebody wanted some they would ride off and he would sell them some in the woods and then move it again. I took all of the marijuana I had and buried it in ammo boxes in the woods and did the same when people wanted some. But what we did to give the impression that we had changed our ways was to put up a chain link fence in the front yard with a big gate and lock. And we left it locked all the time and made a secret entrance to the house through the pine trees. So it looked as if we were never home or that no one was coming or going, and we did cut out a lot of our traffic with the gate. But it was still business as usual for everyone we were close to.

So you can see that the power of this addiction and lifestyle is very strong. Even with the fear of facing the jail time or all the other fears that go along with selling and buying drugs, I would not even think of quitting.

This lifestyle of mine went on with very heavy drug use. I once went on a cocaine binge for ten days straight where just one friend and I snorted four and one half to five grams of cocaine every day. I lost ten pounds or more and looked like death, at least that was what I was told. We did more the eleventh day but only about a gram or so. But I usually did a couple of eight balls every weekend anyway; this was just my longest period without a day in between. Usually every weekend for years I would smoke a half-ounce to an ounce or more of weed per day and would always drink and usually take some kind of pill.

When we were really into ecstasy, me and one friend of mine ate, between the two of us, 26 hits and they were double-stacks, which means two-in-one. That weekend was very long because I did not sleep from the Friday morning I woke up until very early Monday morning. That same weekend I smoked weed and did cocaine along with drinking just to go with all the ecstasy. It is amazing. I tell people all the time that I am not mentally messed up. If you take three hits of acid in your lifetime I've heard it said that you are mentally insane. This goes for ecstasy too. So the fact that I can still put a sentence together is a miracle, because, in all honesty, I have eaten hundreds of hits of ecstasy and a lot of acid, and smoked no telling how much weed along with ounces upon ounces of cocaine, and who knows how much liquor to boot.

Chapter Four

Body Wearing Down, But Still in Bondage!

All the time this is going on, I actually had no intention of even wanting to change. I had slowed down on the cocaine and ecstasy use because, through all the years of my addictions, I was having to constantly battle sickness in my leg due to the heavy drug use. Because of the poor circulation in my blood and more so in my lymphatic system, germs or bacteria that got into my body would not get filtered out as easily as in someone with normal circulation. If the bacteria did not get filtered and settled in an area of my leg, it would cause a very painful infection. The doctors deemed it to be cellulitis infection. This would cause my already purple leg to turn dark red and would bring about pain to a level 10, along with high fever. I ended up having so many bouts with cellulitis that I was hospitalized numerous times. Which also led to me being let go from a job I had helped at for months.

After a two or three day hospitalization and a couple more days at home to recuperate, I returned to work and was shortly let go after they had enough time to act like it wasn't because of the sickness causing me to miss work. I am not bitter but I'm pretty sure of this. I did quickly get another job but the cellulitis caused me to have to quit this one. My doctor told me to just file for disability. I was only 24 when he suggested this.

But I need to back up a couple years. That is just how bad these infections were. So throw that into years of drug abuse and alcoholism. Not only did I have hangovers, blackouts, and times of feeling retarded, I was also constantly dealing with infection in my body, with lots of pain. I figured that the cocaine was really messing me up and not helping to stop the infection. I know I'm a genius, right? So I was actually starting to cut out my cocaine habit. I actually didn't snort cocaine for a few months. There is one thing I hadn't mentioned though, I did have enough head knowledge about Jesus that each night when I would feel like I was about to come out of my body and my heart was about to either stop or explode, I would pray to Jesus and ask for help and ask Him to help me quit. I never told anyone about those prayers though. They were desperate prayers in times when I thought I might actually die. And I truly believe God was starting to work in me or I never would have been able to slow down.

But even though I was slowing down on the cocaine, I had literally no intention of ever quitting smoking weed. I literally joked about being eighty-years old and still smoking weed on my front porch with my friends. By now though, I was slowing down and not looking for those powder parties anymore. I could smoke my weed and still go to bed and get up in the mornings and do the things I liked to do. With the cocaine I couldn't sleep or eat or enjoy hardly anything. So I was getting off of that but was in no way letting go of my weed or the mixed drinks.

The last time I snorted any cocaine was at a New Year's party on December 31, 2001. I hit about two lines after I had not snorted any for a few months, and I really wished I hadn't done it. But I wasn't staying at this party very long. I was waiting on my girlfriend of two years, Dell, to come and pick me up. She got off of work and came by and got me and we left, but I continued to drink and smoke weed the rest of the night.

Now my girlfriend was a very good girl and did not get into the drug scene with me. She was worth quitting drugs, but I was so bound up that the entire time we were dating that I never even slowed down. My life was centered on drugs and I did not know how to live without them.

Now after the New Year's party to bring in 2002, I did not want to snort any more. But I was continually smoking weed. My body was actually becoming so beat down, after all of my hard living, that I was actually starting to quit smoking cigarettes too. But through it all I was holding on to my weed. My cigarette habit had been a bad one too. I sometimes smoked up to four packs a day along with ecstasy and weed. I smoked weed and cigarettes every day for many, many years.

Chapter Five

My Real Encounter With Jesus

Early on in 2002, my mom's church, which was a small group of people meeting in a couple of trailers, was planning to have a revival meeting. My mom stopped by my house to invite me to the revival. I had never been to this church and I, really at the time, did not love my mom either. These couple of things, along with the fact that I didn't want anything to do with church because I was still constantly smoking weed, caused me, needless to say, to be in a state of avoidance. I was going to just let these few days come and go and then there would be no more pressure to go back to church.

You see, I went to church all of my childhood. But once I was old enough and messed up enough, I did not want to play with God. I knew I was bad, so I stayed home. And besides my grandma there was only one man from my church that ever came by my house and lovingly invited me back and shared that everyone missed me. So most of the time I didn't even have any pressure on me to go to church.

My mom and one of my cousins started to put the pressure on me and I thought I knew how these small town revivals went. Usually they would call it revival, which means to bring life back to something that is dead, but it would only be two or three days of special meetings with a rip roaring preacher who was a little louder than your usual preacher, and then things would go back to normal. So I thought I would just avoid the week and then the pressure would be off. But I didn't know how much God loved me, and all the others in our region. I didn't know that God was about to change my life for real and for good.

The week of revival came and went and I thought, well, that is over. But my mom came back over and said that revival went so good that they were going to extend it another week. Yippee! Yeah right, I was not at all happy about that. This was just more aggravation to me. So I weaseled out of the next week too. But to my surprise my mom came back again and said it is going so good we are going another week. I couldn't believe this. I had never heard of it before. I mean a revival that actually revived people and that stirred people to the point that they wanted to keep going to church on days that were not the regularly scheduled days. I was amazed and again aggravated at the same time.

So one day came and I was with some friends smoking blunts around the pool, and I had decided to go to church that night. I was going to ride with one of my cousins. If I had drove I would not have made it there, I'm sure. I would have been detoured. I joked while smoking the weed about having to go that night. But when the time came I went, earrings, tattoos and all.

When I got there I knew a ton of people and they were so glad to see me because they knew that God was changing lives. And if anybody needed a life change it was me. It was like I was going 90 miles an hour in the wrong direction.

So anyway, I was there, but was very uncomfortable and I sat towards the back. The preacher was a fiery man of God from the islands of Trinidad. He began to preach and I cannot remember a thing he said that night but whatever he said it was causing God, the Holy Spirit, to convict me and draw me, and I was under the influence of the PRESENCE OF GOD, and it was more powerful than the weed I had been smoking earlier in the day, that was for sure. All I know is when he gave an invitation for us to give our lives to Jesus and be forgiven of our sins, I knew I needed that. So I raised my hand to show him I wanted to pray and accept Jesus and be forgiven. I already had head knowledge of the Gospel message about Jesus and His sacrificial love and death and resurrection. But now I was getting the heart knowledge. That preacher used to say that some people miss heaven by twelve inches, the distance between their head and their heart. I was getting my heart right and accepting Jesus' forgiveness and His sacrifice. I remember ladies that had seen me grow up coming over crying and hugging me, I was crying too. I thought I was hard, but I was broken in the Presence of God. Jesus was loving on me and purging me, and I was just as broken as I could be.

The preacher came to the back where I was and prayed with me. He had never met me, but I think everyone had told him about me, and he knew this was a miracle of God that I came and was saved. He laid his hands on me and prayed for me. I felt a physical weight come off of me. It felt like it lifted off of my shoulders and I knew I was saved!

It was really amazing. I felt so good and so sure I had been saved by the Blood of Jesus that on the way home in the car I said, "You can hit the ditch, I know where I'm going." Can you believe it, I was so certain I had been saved that at that moment I didn't care if my life ended anymore because I was sure of where I would be going. And PRAISE GOD, I AM STILL SURE!

While all of this is happening, I had a friend living with me at my house. I got him smoking weed and hooked him up with my cocaine connection, so he sold powder and I sold the weed. Together we had most anybody covered with whatever they wanted, drug wise. Well, he didn't go with me to church that night and I wasn't planning on anything happening to me anyway, so when I got home it was my first test and a shocker for my friend.

I walked in the door and my friend was waiting for me. He had a big fat joint rolled up, what we called a hog leg. I felt so good and so clean, and the time I walk in there is my best friend standing in the kitchen waiting for me with what was my usual favorite.

He mockingly asked, "Well, did you have fun at church?"

I replied, "Yea, I did."

He said, "Well, do you want to smoke one?"

I said, "No, I don't." I told him I got saved. And I walked right by him holding the fat joint and I went to my room and shut the door. This shocked my friend. He had literally never seen me turn down a joint, ever. So when I didn't smoke the thing this really impacted him. I don't know what he did that night to this day. But I know that in just two weeks of me continuing to go to the revival meetings, which by the way lasted a total of ten weeks with over 400 people saved, and sharing with him what I saw God do each night, he gave his life to Jesus in the dope house!

After we both committed our lives to Jesus, he returned to the church he grew up in and was baptized shortly after. And we began to clean house, literally. I had lots of weed and several bongs and pipes. Not to mention we had 75 clone plants growing in my barn that we had been taking care of and they were rooted and ready to be planted. We were about to make thousands of dollars on them. So we gathered up all the pipes and bongs and took them to the dumpster and began to slam them and brake them in the dumpster! We slammed and broke the things of our past life and we were beginning our new lives. We gave the plants back to the guy who hooked us up with them and we told him we didn't want any money. We didn't want anything to do with drugs or that lifestyle any more! Jesus had completely changed our lives! I threw away CD's, movies, and anything else that had anything to do with my old way of life.

Chapter Six

Surprise! You Still Have to Reap What You Sow!

After I got saved, I took my girlfriend, Dell, to church with me too. The first time she went she rededicated her life and was powerfully touched by God. So now our relationship was getting better. Where my life had revolved around dope and had her in it, I really wasn't a very good boyfriend, but now it was beginning to revolve around Jesus, and this was very beneficial to our relationship as well.

So we began to go to church regularly. I started reading my Bible that my dad had given me years earlier. As a teenager I used to just leave it at church, but now I kept it with me everywhere I went.

Though we were doing a lot better, there was still sin in our lives and we had sown a lot of bad seed in certain areas that would be very evident soon. The Bible says in Galatians 6:7, "Do not be deceived, God is not mocked; for whatever a man sows, that he will also reap." And I know this to be true.

We had been having an immoral relationship and soon after we had both given our lives to Jesus, we found out that my girlfriend, Dell, was pregnant. We found out you still have to reap what you sow.

But the LORD had done a work in our hearts and even though we had some fear and concerns about our new situation, we knew we wanted to do the right things. We had been together for over two years and I had been blessed even in my sinful life with a house, so we planned a quick wedding and got married on my 24th birthday, April 20, 2002.

There is always mercy and grace available to everyone and in every situation. Do not let anyone tell you different. As long as you are alive and breathing you are a candidate to receive God's mercy and grace in your life, and the Blood of Jesus is more than enough to cleanse you and make you whole!

1 John 1:9 states that "If we confess our sins, He is faithful and just to forgive us our sins and to cleanse us from all unrighteousness." Jesus is faithful and just to forgive us of our sins and to cleanse us, HALLELUJAH! That is the good news I needed. And that is the good news everyone needs to hear, that Jesus is not out to get us in a bad way, but He is out to get us and to bring us back to our Father who created us and to bring us into a relationship with Him and into His righteousness.

2 Cor. 5:19 (NLT) states, "For God was in Christ, reconciling the world to himself, no longer counting people's sins against them. This is the wonderful message he has given us to tell others."

So now, after receiving salvation, we also received mercy and grace. Now we were married and my friend who was my roommate moved in with my mom and brother. And PRAISE GOD, I moved in my new wife! This was a much better arrangement. What an understatement!

Now my wife and I began to really start pursuing the LORD, and at the same time had a little one on the way. At the time I was praying hard for a boy, because I had been the bad guy after other "daddy's little girls", and this was my biggest fear. I thought if I have a girl, I am going to have to kill somebody or get killed some day. I hope that all dads would have so much love for their children and pray that they would never actually kill anyone, but that they would cherish their children enough to show them the love that our God showed us.

John 15:13 says, "Greater love has no one than this, than to lay down one's life for his friends."

Romans 5:6 states that "For when we were still without strength, in due time Christ died for the ungodly."

Romans 5:8 says, "But God demonstrates His own love toward us, in that while we were still sinners, Christ died for us."

God answered my prayer and gave us a son, Thomas Kaiser Jackson. Now I feel like I understand and relate to God a little bit better since I, too, have a son, and he is my one and only son. During the pregnancy we were in church all the time. We went on Sundays like everybody else and we went on Mondays for prayer meeting. And this was a genuine prayer meeting, all we did was come in and get on our faces before the LORD and pray. We had the lights down low and all you could hear were the prayers of others in the distance all over the church. Not many attended but this was always the most powerful time of encounter with God we had at church. We also went on Tuesday night, which was our mid-week service. We met on Tuesday instead of Wednesday to try to break out of the religious mold and give others a chance to visit with us and not compromise their church attendance. This has turned out to be a very smart move.

Along with our 4 services a week, we also did many outreaches. My wife and I were very faithful to help out and attended most every meeting. We were soon plugged in to help out in every way we could, which wasn't a lot, but we did what we could.

Chapter Seven

More Grace and the Baptism of the Holy Spirit

Now we had completely given our lives to Jesus, I mean we were not perfect, and still aren't, but our lives revolve around Jesus and the things of God. So we both were genuinely seeking the LORD and wanting to get closer to Him. We were hungry for MORE OF HIM. This is very important for all Christians, to stay hungry for Him, and to stay desperate for MORE of His PRESENCE and His GLORY. Without the manifest power of God in our lives people will not be changed.

So as we were becoming accustomed to our church doing another outreach, Dell and I were getting involved in it as much as we could. I was actually going to be in a dance or drama type of ministry with some young guys. We were in the LORD'S army. We were wearing camouflage and were being very militant. I think it went good, not because of me or my talent, or lack of talent, but because our hearts were pure and we were being obedient.

In one of these meetings, there were about three, I can remember my wife being great with child. I am not sure of the date or exact meeting, but I remember we were so happy and content in our hearts, but we were still hungry for and open to God and whatever He had for us. This one night we had a team of brothers leading worship, The Miller Brothers from Florida, and we were all having a great time. My pastor had preached and people had gotten saved, and they were having some ministry time and more altar service for anyone who wanted to pray or be prayed for. I told my wife we don't really need anything but let's just go down and pray. There were some other pastors there from other towns that were friends with our pastor. They were a great bunch of guys and were full of the FIRE OF GOD!

We went down and began to pray just standing there open to whatever God had for us. As we prayed, a couple of the other pastors came up to me and laid their hands on me. One in particular, was Pastor Jimmy Boatright from Baxley, Georgia. I will never forget him and how God used him this night. At the time I was not personally acquainted with him but I knew who he was. He came up to me and put his hands on my stomach and began to pray for me, and the moment his hand touched my stomach, I felt power come into my stomach and all over my body. I could no longer stand up. I found myself falling to the floor under the Power of God! I was totally conscious. I could hear the singing and could see everyone and everything going on around me, but all of a sudden, I was overcome and overshadowed by the Power of God, and I was physically stuck to the floor! I felt like I had a knot in my stomach, and a knot in my neck, and I physically could not get myself up off of the floor! It did not hurt but I could not break free from this powerful touch!

As I was on the floor, like I said, I was totally conscious, so while those same pastors were praying for others I would reach over and lay my hand on their legs to help them pray for others. As if they needed my help, but looking back that was and is still my heart, to pray and see God touch others the way He touched me. When the other pastors felt my hand touch their leg, they turned around as quick as they could and laid hands on me again! This happened two or three times and every time they laid their hands on me I could feel that same power increase on and in me again. After awhile the only thing I could and was doing was lying on that theater floor with both of my hands lifted up to Heaven and crying and praising God. To this day I do not know how long I was stuck to the floor. I do know that I was there so long that when I was able to get up, the singers had already quit singing, and were gone, and that everyone else had already left the building too except for some people from my church who were waiting it out with me. I'm glad they did because when I got up I had held my hands up for so long that all the blood had left them and when I stood up I almost passed out. I had to sit down in one of the seats. I sat long enough to regain my composure. Then I was able to get up and walk. This is when I was baptized with the Holy Spirit. My life had already been changed, but from that moment on it was changed again and even more. HALLELUJAH!

There is a baptism with the Holy Spirit. Here is what the Bible says about it and what God has taught me since my encounter on that awesome night.

Baptism of the Holy Ghost

Jesus is the Baptizer in the Holy Ghost. Here is John the Baptists' testimony to Jesus as the baptizer of the Holy Ghost.

Matt 3:11, "I indeed baptize you with water unto repentance, but He who is coming after me is mightier that I, whose sandals I am not worthy to carry. He will baptize you with the Holy Spirit and fire."

Mark 1:7-8, "And he preached, saying, 'There comes One after me who is mightier than I, whose sandals strap I am not worthy to stoop down and loose. I indeed baptized you with water, but He will baptize you with the Holy Spirit.'"

Luke 3:16, "John answered, saying to all, 'I indeed baptize you with water; but One mightier than I is coming, whose sandal strap I am not worthy to loose. He will baptize you with the Holy Spirit and fire.'"

John has another proclamation of the One to come after Him but there is another couple of scriptures I want to share that also reference this baptism.

Luke 11:13, "If you then being evil know how to give good gifts to your children, how much more will your heavenly Father give the Holy Spirit to those who ask Him!"

John 14:21, "He who has My commandments and keeps them, it is he who loves Me. And he who loves Me will be loved by My Father, and I will love him and manifest Myself to him."

John 1:33, "I did not know Him, but He who sent me to baptize with water said to me, "Upon whom you see the Spirit descending, and remaining on Him, this is He who baptizes with the Holy Spirit."

John 7:37-39 (MESSAGE), "On the final and climactic day of the Feast, Jesus took his stand. He cried out, 'If anyone thirsts, let him come to me and drink. Rivers of living water will brim and spill out of the depths of anyone who believes in me this way, just as the Scripture says.'" (He said this in regard to the Spirit, whom those who believed in him were about to receive. The Spirit had not yet been given because Jesus had not yet been glorified.)

But PRAISE GOD, NOW HE HAS BEEN GLORIFIED AND THE SPIRIT HAS BEEN GIVEN! If we believe in Jesus then let's receive what He has for us, the baptism of the Holy Spirit! There is not a formula or a set of certain motions to go through to receive this baptism. There are just a few must haves:

YOU MUST BELIEVE IN THE LORD JESUS AND BE SAVED.
YOU MUST SURRENDER YOUR LIFE TO HIM.
YOU MUST BE OPEN TO WHATEVER GOD HAS FOR YOU.
YOU MUST BE HUNGRY FOR EVERYTHING HE HAS TO OFFER.
YOU MUST GET OUT OF YOUR HEAD TRYING TO FIGURE GOD OUT AND OPEN YOUR HEART.
YOU MUST YIELD TO THE HOLY SPIRIT.

I'll give you some Biblical examples of how it has happened.

Acts 1:4-5, "And being assembled together with them, he commanded them not to depart from Jerusalem, but to wait for the promise of the Father, "which," He said, "You have heard from Me; for John truly baptized with water, but you shall be baptized with the Holy Spirit not many days from now."

Acts 1:8, "But you shall receive power after the Holy Spirit has come upon you; and you will be witnesses to Me in Jerusalem and in all of Judea and Samaria, and to the end of the earth."

Acts 2:1-4, "When the Day of Pentecost had fully come, they were all with one accord in one place. And suddenly there came a sound from heaven, as of a rushing mighty wind, and it filled the whole house where they were sitting. Then there appeared to them divided tongues as of fire, and one sat upon each of them. And they were all filled with the Holy Spirit and began to speak with other tongues, as the Spirit gave them utterance."

Acts 2:12-18, "So they were all amazed and perplexed, saying to one another, whatever could this mean? Others mocking said, 'They are full of new wine.' But Peter, standing up with the eleven, raised his voice and said to them, 'Men and women of Judea and all who dwell in Jerusalem, let this be known to you, and heed my words. For these are not drunk, as you suppose, since it is only the third hour of the day. But this is what was spoken by the prophet Joel: And it shall come to pass in the last days, says God, that I will pour out of My Spirit on all flesh; your sons and your daughters shall prophesy, your young men shall see visions, your old men shall dream dreams. And on My menservants and on My maidservants I will pour out My Spirit in those days; and they shall prophesy.'"

Acts 2:38-39, "Then Peter said to them, "Repent, and let every one of you be baptized in the name of Jesus Christ for the remission of sins; and you shall receive the gift of the Holy Spirit. For the promise is to you and to your children, and to all who are afar off, as many as the Lord our God will call."

You can receive by hearing the word or by the laying on of hands. And when you receive you might cry, you might laugh, you might fall out, you might shake, and you might get stuck to the floor. You might be conscious or you might be unconscious. Either way it is God's touch. On the Day of Pentecost everyone looked drunk!

Here are some more scriptural references. The Bible is the Inspired Word of God and IS ABSOLUTE TRUTH. So do not believe just because I tell you of my experience, but believe because God's word is truth. All of our experiences must line up with the Word of God.

Acts 8:14-17, "Now when the apostles who were at Jerusalem heard that Samaria had received the word of God, they sent Peter and John to them, who, when they had come down, prayed for them that they might receive the Holy Spirit. For as yet He had fallen upon none of them. They had only been baptized in the name of the Lord Jesus. Then they laid hands on them, and they received the Holy Spirit."

This text should settle any argument about the fact that the baptism with the Holy Spirit happens automatically when we are saved. These people of Samaria had received the word of God and not only believed but had also been baptized in the name of the Lord Jesus, but had not been baptized with the Holy Spirit. Holy Spirit hadn't fallen on any of them yet. So they sent Peter and John specifically for them to pray that they would receive the Holy Spirit. If this were automatic there would have been no need for them to go and pray, it would have been done already. But this baptism is another blessing and it is needed.

Jesus told the disciples before He ascended not to depart until they had received this power from on high. This must be a crucial and vital part of our spiritual lives. I believe the baptism with the Holy Spirit is totally necessary for us to be the men and women of God that the Father is calling us to be. If Peter and John needed it then I know I need it. And I want it! And I have it! PRAISE GOD! And you need it and can have it too.

Acts 9:17-18, "And Ananias went his way and entered the house; and laying his hands on him he said, 'Brother Saul, the Lord Jesus, who appeared to you on the road as you came, has sent me that you may receive your sight and be filled with the Holy Spirit.' Immediately there fell from his eyes something like scales, and he received his sight at once; and he arose and was baptized."

The fact that the scales fell off of his eyes is also the proof that he was filled or baptized with the Holy Spirit. There is an example of Jesus doing something in the Spirit that is invisible but the proof that the invisible spiritual work has been done is proven by the physical visible work that is done.

When Ananias said that you may receive your sight and be filled with the Holy Spirit, look at what happened. He laid his hands on him and something like scales fell from his eyes. The fact that he received his sight proves that he was also filled with the Spirit. Let's look at another scripture to prove this.

Mark 2:1-12, "And again He entered Capernaum after some days, and it was heard that He was in the house. Immediately many gathered together, so that there was no longer room to receive them, not even near the door. And he preached the word to them. Then they came to Him, bringing a paralytic who was carried by four men. And when they could not come near Him because of the crowd, they uncovered the roof where He was. So when they had broken through, they let down the bed on which the paralytic was lying. When Jesus saw their faith, He said to the paralytic, 'Son, your sins are forgiven you.' And some of the scribes were sitting there and reasoning in their hearts, 'Why does this Man speak blasphemies like this? Who can forgive sins but God alone?' But immediately, when Jesus perceived in His Spirit that they reasoned thus within themselves, He said to them, 'Why do you reason about these things in your hearts? Which is easier, to say to the paralytic, 'Your sins are forgiven you,' or to say, 'Arise, take up your bed and walk'? But that you may know that the Son of Man has power on earth to forgive sins.' He said to the paralytic, 'I say to you, arise take up your bed, and go to your house.' Immediately he arose, took up the bed, and went out in the presence of them all, so that they all were amazed and glorified God, saying, 'We never saw anything like this!'"

Jesus proved that He had power on earth to forgive sins, an invisible Spiritual work. He proved that the paralytic's sins were truly forgiven by working a visible, physical miracle. The miracle confirmed His word was and is true.

In this same way, Paul received the Spirit because it was the word of the LORD, and the scales falling off of his eyes confirmed it.

Now let's look at some more scriptures to confirm the baptism with the Holy Spirit.

Acts 10:44-47, "While Peter was still speaking these words, the Holy Spirit fell upon all those who heard the word. And those of the circumcision who believed were astonished, as many as came with Peter, because the gift of the Holy Spirit had been poured out on the Gentiles also. For they heard them speak with tongues and magnify God. Then Peter answered, 'Can anyone forbid water, that these should not be baptized who have received the Holy Spirit just as we have?'"

This is an awesome passage! We have now seen that you can receive the baptism of the Holy Spirit by the laying on of hands and now by just preaching the word! "While Peter was still speaking, the Holy Spirit fell upon those who heard the word." That is amazing!

And we need to pay attention to what happened when the Holy Spirit fell upon them. They heard them speak with tongues and magnify God, and Peter said that they had "received the Holy Spirit just as we have," and we read in Acts chapter two what happened to them, they spoke with tongues and some thought that they were drunk. So we need to realize that when we truly encounter Jesus and God the Holy Spirit, that we will leave amazed, and we will be able to say what they said in Mark 2:17, "We never saw anything like this!"

And God is so amazing and He is so huge and complex that I truly believe that He never has to duplicate Himself or His touch. He may manifest some of the same healings or miracles, but I truly believe that we can get into His presence a million times or more and He would be able to show us a new facet of whom He is. He never has to duplicate!

Acts 11:15-17, "And as I began to speak, the Holy Spirit fell upon them, as upon us at the beginning. Then I remembered the word of the Lord, how He said, 'John indeed baptized with water, but you shall be baptized with the Holy Spirit.' If therefore God gave them the same gift as He gave us when we believed on the Lord Jesus Christ, who was I that I could withstand God?"

And just like Peter said that day, I say it to all who would refute the word of God today. Who are we that we can withstand God? If God chooses to give people today the same gift that He gave the 120 disciples when they believed on the day of Pentecost, who are we to withstand Him and what He chooses to do? Peter had sense enough to accept it and rejoice in it. I hope we all have that much sense.

Acts 19:1-7, "And it happened, while Apollos was at Corinth, that Paul, having passed through the upper regions, came to Ephesus. And finding some disciples he said to them, 'Did you receive the Holy Spirit when you believed?' So they said to him, 'We have not so much as heard whether there is a Holy Spirit.' And he said to them, 'Into what then were you baptized?' So they said, 'Into John's baptism.' Then Paul said, 'John indeed baptized with a baptism of repentance, saying to the people that they should believe on Him who would come after him, that is, on Christ Jesus.' When they heard this, they were baptized in the name of the Lord Jesus. And when Paul had laid hands on them, the Holy Spirit came upon them, and they spoke with tongues and prophesied. Now the men were about twelve in all."

Now I already know that this topic is one of the most misunderstood and debated topics of all of scripture, but God has shown us in His word this is what would and did happen when His church was born, and I have found it to be a vital part to staying on fire for Him, and a great gift to help us stay in communion. I am very thankful to Jesus Christ my LORD and SAVIOR for blessing me with salvation and the baptism of the Holy Spirit.

I grew up in a denomination that does not teach on the subject and who many of the churches, not all, but many do not accept or believe that this still happens. The scripture itself should be enough evidence. And there are literally millions of believers who have experienced this baptism.

My beautiful wife was so far along in her pregnancy when I received the Baptism that I'm glad she didn't at the time because if she had fallen under the power some of us would have been scared to death. But God is in control and always has a plan.

After Dell had our son Kaiser, which she had with no complications whatsoever, PRAISE GOD! She was seeking the LORD too. We were very faithful. And God was honoring our faith every day. But the night came when our pastor invited our friend, Pastor Jimmy Boatright. He began to minister on the baptism of the Holy Spirit and my wife was stirred up. She was already praying to receive, but with
the same pastor who had prayed for me when I received at our church, her faith was stirred even more. We knew that he was full of the fire of God. So he began to preach, and in the

beginning, he asked a show of hands for who wanted to receive the baptism of the Holy Ghost and to receive the prayer language. My wife and several others raised their hands.

When the time came for the people to put their faith in action and go up to receive, he invited them to come to the front and was going to lay his hands on them the same way Paul had done in the Bible. No one went up front but Dell. He was amazed that almost everyone had chickened out. But my wife was there and God was ready to pour out His Spirit.

When he laid his hands on Dell she went out under the power just as quick as his hand touched her head. She began to speak in tongues very fast. This had never happened to her before. She was caught but laid out on the floor speaking in tongues very fast and very loud, which if you know my wife is very out of character for her. That is why we know this was God because when He touches you, you will not be the same person you have been. You will be completely changed from the inside out!

2 Cor. 5:17, "Therefore, if anyone is in Christ, he is a new creation; old things have passed away; behold, all things have become new."

Now after Dell was waxed, as we jokingly say, totally wrecked by God's power, it stirred the others up who had chickened out. Others went up to receive and they did too. But the most amazing part of the night was that whenever someone else was receiving, Dell would get even louder and even faster in her tongues! She was out in the Spirit lying flat on the floor speaking in tongues and getting louder and faster! It was amazing! And God wasn't through rocking our finite minds yet.

Dell's dad had been very sick around this time and he was weighing heavy on her heart. She had been in much prayer for him, she is continually covering her family, and she prays more than she gives herself credit for. She is so important to me and for me to have in my life. But after we left the service her mom called her up and asked her if she had been praying for her daddy. She replied no, not that night, and then it hit her that she might have been praying for her daddy in the Spirit. She called because he felt like someone was praying for him while he was sitting at home! She asked what time he felt like that and when he told her she knew it was the same time she was on the floor praying in the Spirit! If you don't believe, you have come to late to tell me, because I know! God proved Himself that night and changed us!

In 1 Corinthians 2:9-14, the Bible reveals to us how our spirit knows more about us than we know about ourselves. "The natural man does not receive the things of the Spirit for they are foolishness to him;" we must be led by the Spirit of God or we will miss out on some of the most important things in our lives.

You see, what happened that night all happened in the Spirit. Dell was baptized in the Holy Spirit, and her spirit knew the most important things in her heart, the deep things. Her spirit knew the importance of the situation her daddy was in. And when she surrendered her body and her tongue to the LORD, her spirit began to intercede for her daddy. At that moment, her daddy's condition wasn't on her mind, but it was weighing heavy on her spirit. And the spirit searched out those deep things and began to pray for them, and the effect of that prayer was felt instantly! PRAISE GOD for the baptism of the Holy Spirit and for the ability to pray in the Spirit!

Jude 20, "But you, beloved, building yourselves up on your most holy faith, praying in the Holy Spirit."

That is your most holy faith, praying in the Holy Spirit.

But the baptism of the Holy Spirit is not all there is. We are to be continually filled with the Spirit. This baptism is our preparation and where we receive power.

Acts 1:8, "But you shall receive power when the Holy Spirit comes upon you." This power is so vital for ministry. Paul had it and so did all the others who God birthed the church through, so if they needed it so do we.

1 Thessalonians 1:5, "For our gospel did not come to you in word only, but also in power, and in the Holy Spirit."

I Corinthians 2:4-5, "And my speech and my preaching were not with persuasive words of human wisdom, but in demonstration of the Spirit and of power, that your faith should not be in the wisdom of men, but in the power of God."

Chapter Eight

The Call of God: Stepping Into God's Plan For My Life

The first months of my new life in God were great, but I had to learn some things. When I was saved the first thing that was on my mind was two of my first cousins, Jesse and Jaye. They were young and in church and I knew that I wanted to set a good example for them now. I had already set a bad one long enough. So I decided to go back to the church that I had grown up in. God would not let me be satisfied there though. Dell and I went back and forth until I knew that God was calling us to China Hill Christian Church, the church I had been saved at.

This was a difficult situation because, in south Georgia, most people don't go to church where God calls them; they just go where their family went, so for people to leave one church and go to another is a rare thing. But I knew that God was calling me to leave and I knew where He wanted me to be. This became evident very soon.

Once we really plugged into the new church, God began to use us to help out in all kinds of ways. We were as faithful as we could be, and we learned that God honors your faithfulness. Faithfulness really means a lot to Him. Even if we are not the most anointed or know the most amounts of scripture, He will simply honor a person whose heart is truly faithful.

Matt 25:23, "His lord said to him, 'Well done, good and faithful servant; you have been faithful over a few things, I will make you ruler over many things. Enter into the joy of your lord.'"

Luke 19:17, "And he said to him, 'Well done, good servant; because you were faithful in a very little, have authority over ten cities.'"

As time went on, I fell in love with the Word of God. When our son Kaiser was born, my wife, Dell, stayed home with him and kept a couple of other babies until he was a little over a year old, and then I came out of work and started to stay home and keep Him. Those days while he was a baby, he would sleep late and would take naps too. Those were the days. While he slept a lot I can remember sitting in my chair and reading and praying about two hours every morning and every day getting to read and pray another two during lunchtime while he napped again. And some of those naps went from two to four hours.

So every day I was in the Word of God and prayer, anywhere from four to six hours a day! I didn't realize it yet but God was preparing me for ministry and He was doing it in overdrive.

After only about four or five months of being saved, our pastor set my good friend over the teenagers in our church and he began to minister to our youth. He appointed me as an understudy or apprentice, which was a good idea since my friend was several years older than me, and we worked well together too. But as time went on I found myself beginning to start preaching to myself. I would go by a mirror and preach myself saved again and again! I started preaching to myself all the time and my heart began to yearn to want to preach.

In youth meetings, while my friend would be ministering, I would find myself thinking, "You should say this or should say it like that." I was feeling the call to the ministry. This call was burning in my heart and in my spirit. I felt inside that I was supposed to be leading the teenagers in our church, but I didn't want to say anything and I didn't know what to do but to just keep doing what I had been doing.

The opportunity did finally come for me to preach at my own church on a Tuesday night! I was so excited and had been studying for months now, and God had shown me so many things. I can remember that night; there were eighty people there. And at our church, that was at the time a doublewide trailer completely gutted out and turned into a sanctuary, that was a packed house. This was the first night I would get to preach, and I felt right at home. All the people were excited because they had just recently seen the hand of God change my life and this was the work He was continuing to do.

My pastor told me to speak for twenty minutes, but once I got going I was so full of the Word and excitement that I preached for fifty! But the people weren't mad or tired, God really anointed me that night and we laughed and cried and rejoiced in the LORD! So once I had a taste of this, I was even more certain that this was my calling in life. It is a wonderful feeling to find your purpose in life and begin to step into it and work towards perfecting it.

The great news is that God has a purpose and a plan for all of us!

Jeremiah 29:11, "For I know the plans I have for you," declares the Lord, "plans to prosper you and not to harm you, plans to give you hope and a future."

Soon after that, I was really feeling the call to take over the youth ministry. I would tell Dell how I was feeling. I can remember telling her I just knew I was supposed to be leading those teenagers. My heart was yearning to reach them and to lead them. God really placed a special anointing on me for them and gave me a heart for them. This is not a unique thing; He does this for everyone He calls. If He doesn't give you a heart and a desire for the people you are ministering to then you might need to reevaluate why you are ministering. You must have a heart for the people you minister to. A good leader will be willing to lay down his life for the sheep of his flock. Moses taught us that lesson as well as Jesus.

Moses had such a heart for the children of Israel that he killed an Egyptian that was beating one of them. And later, even after the golden calf incident, he tried to make atonement for their sin himself, and even offered his own life if God would spare them. Now that is a heart for the people!

Exodus 2:11, "Now it came to pass in those days, when Moses was grown, that he went out to his brethren and looked at their burdens. And he saw an Egyptian beating a Hebrew, one of his brethren. So he looked this way and that way, and when he saw no one, he killed the Egyptian and hid him in the sand."

Exodus 32:1-9, "Now when the people saw that Moses delayed coming down from the mountain, the people gathered together to Aaron, and said to him, 'Come, make us gods that shall go before us; for as for this Moses, the man who brought us up out of the land of Egypt, we do not know what has become of him.' And Aaron said to them, 'Break off the golden earrings which are in the ears of your wives, your sons, and your daughters, and bring them to me.' So all the people broke off the golden earrings which were in their ears, and brought them to Aaron. And he received the gold from their hand, and he fashioned it with an engraving tool, and made a molded calf. Then they said, 'This is your god, O Israel, that brought you out of the land of Egypt!' So when Aaron saw it, he built an altar before it. And Aaron made a proclamation and said, 'Tomorrow is a feast to the LORD.' Then they rose early on the next day, offered burnt offerings, and brought peace offerings; and the people sat down to eat and drink, and rose up to play. And the LORD said to Moses, 'Go, get down! For your people whom you brought out of the land of Egypt have corrupted themselves. They have turned aside quickly out of the way which I commanded them. They have made themselves a molded calf, and worshiped it and sacrificed to it, and said, 'This is your god, O Israel, that brought you out of the land of Egypt!' And the LORD said to Moses, 'I have seen this people, and indeed it is a stiff-necked people!"

And now let's see his reaction for the people even after they had sinned very badly. And we won't forget they did get some harsh punishment, about 3000 people did die. (Exodus 32:25-28). That's harsh.

But God, at that time, was ready to start all over and made Moses the offer of a lifetime, but he refused and began to intercede for the people he was leading. This shows his heart for the people, one that is rarely seen these days, I think.

Exodus 32:10, "Now therefore, let Me alone that My wrath may burn hot against them and I may consume them. And I will make of you a great nation."

Sounds pretty tempting, God offering to make you a great nation. But Moses has such an awesome heart and major character we can all learn from. He was not power hungry or greedy, he just wanted his people to be back in relationship with their God and to get them to the Promised Land so they could worship. What a great heart. God help us become leaders that are not swayed by grand offers but that we be people of great character that only want to see others led to Jesus, and led to worship Him, and to come into true relationship with Him.

Now after Moses comes down and sees the idol and chastens them, we see his heart again.

Exodus 32:30-32, "Now it came to pass on the next day that Moses said to the people, 'You have committed a great sin. So now I will go up to the LORD; perhaps I can make atonement for your sin.' Then Moses returned to the LORD and said, 'Oh, these people have committed a great sin, and have made for themselves a god of gold! Yet now, if You will forgive their sin—but if not, I pray, blot me out of Your book which You have written.'"

Now that is a heart for the people! Moses was willing to completely give up his eternal life for the people of God. I am sure glad God gave him the answer He did. And I am glad that Jesus did come and make atonement for all our sin.

Now as my heart was burning for these teens, and the call was strong in my heart to lead and take over, I really did not know what to do. I only told my wife and I just kept helping and praying and doing the things I was learning to do. But one day God opened a door that, to this day, no man has shut. Our pastor wanted to go visit a fellow who had given his life to Jesus but was struggling. He asked my friend and I, whom he placed over the youth, to go with him. We both were glad to go. We got in the car with him and we all started to ride way out toward our friend's house. I can still remember to this day sitting in the back seat going down some dirt roads.

Our pastor brought up the youth ministry and very casually said he wanted my friend to step down and wanted me to step up. On the outside I played it cool, but on the inside I was doing back flips! I was so happy. I knew this was what God was calling me to do and now he had opened the door and I had never said a word to either of them about it at all. God was really teaching me to be sensitive to His leading and promptings. Even though I didn't know a lot of scriptures or much of anything about ministry, God was showing me my purpose and putting me right in the middle of it. And I couldn't have been happier.

The youth ministry was given to me to do with it whatever I thought needed doing. I wasn't sure what really needed doing at first, but I began to plan meetings about every other week on Saturdays. The couple of things I knew we had to have was pizza and the Presence of God!

In my first meetings we would have six to ten teenagers, and we would hang out eating pizza, and then I would share with them the word that God had showed me that week, and then I would lay hands on them and pray for them. That is all I knew about ministry, but I was on the right track. We added worship music and continued to preach the word and have time for ministry.

It wasn't long before we had a new family join our church. Usually one family joining your church is good but not really worth noting, but this family was different. It was a family that lived only a mile away from my house and I knew the parents pretty well. I was so excited that they came and joined us because they not only were a very spiritual family with a lot to offer, but they had 21 children, and six of them were teenagers! This was great for me because my youth group doubled over night! I went from six to twelve. My ministry was growing and we were now multicultural too.

This family was no ordinary family, it was Billy and Bonnie Walker, the founders of Refuge Ranch. They had three biological children of their own and, after many miscarriages, God moved on them to begin adopting children as their ministry, and there is no one I know that would have been more loving or better for the job. At that time they had twenty-one children, but as I am writing they have adopted five more siblings this week! That ups their total to twenty-six children!

So my ministry was growing and so was I. I began to learn more and more about teenagers and teen ministry. I had been delivered from so much that I could relate to them and get on their level and speak their language. And thanks be to God, I still can. This is a gift from God and it is the call of God on my life. You can work hard and become an effective minister but if the call of God is not on your life for that specific ministry you will not be as effective. It is God's call and anointing that gifts you and prepares you for His service and ministry. I learned this early on in ministry because I didn't have the wealth of scripture knowledge that I heard other people have. And I was not trained in any ministry school or teaching. But I had the call of God and a heart to minister. This proved to be enough for God, although it isn't for a lot of people.

From the very beginning of my ministry God's power was there. Even though I wasn't seminary trained when I laid my hands on the teenagers, God's power would overtake them and they would fall out under His power. I sought for and wanted God's power from the beginning of my ministry until now because I saw that if it was up to me or any other person to change lives it would not happen, but if God's power was there, lives would be changed forever! I know mine was, and it was not changed by a man's story but by God's power! So, early on, I learned to depend on God, the Holy Spirit, to lead me, and for His presence and power to come every time I was allowed to minister.

1 Corinthians 2:4-5, "And my speech and my preaching were not with persuasive words of human wisdom, but in demonstration of the Spirit and of power, that your faith should not be in the wisdom of men but in the power of God."

As time went on I learned more and became better and better at communicating and reaching the lost. I saw many, every time I shared my testimony, come to know Jesus. It seemed as though if there was one that didn't know Jesus as their Savior, I would try to reach them and did reach them very often. I began to be used by God to become a fruitful evangelist. God opened many doors for me at other churches and I was used by Him to lead more to the LORD.

Soon our youth ministry had grown more and we were having meetings every week instead of every other. Our church met on Tuesday nights instead of Wednesday, like most all the other churches in our region. Our pastor didn't let me have a meeting during our regular scheduled days, so my wife and I had to go another day just for the teenagers. We chose Wednesday night to meet with the teens and God blessed it. We have always picked up whoever wanted to go and took them to the youth meetings.

Our attendance grew and our influence was continuing to grow. We were seeing God save more teenagers from drugs and alcohol. I began to raise up leaders, we started a dance ministry, and were blessed to go to different churches in our community and minister to them through dance and preaching.

With our church miles away from any city, and the cities we were close to were very small, we still had about 40 teens coming out from miles around. And the power of God would touch them and change them. It was an awesome learning time and time of ministry. But in my heart was a desire to reach more and to do more. It seemed so difficult when we all had to come from so far, and most of the ones we ministered to didn't have a driver's license or a vehicle. But my passion for Jesus was ever increasing and I was determined to continue to stay the course and keep ministering no matter how many we had.

Chapter Nine

My Heart for Worship

The reason I became so dedicated to the LORD was because I realized how bad I was and how much mercy and grace He had shown to me.

Romans 5:20, "But where sin abounded, grace abounded much more."

I realized the price Jesus paid for me and that I had done nothing worthy of Him to die for me. I realized that I didn't even choose Him, He chose me. It is hard for me to believe that He would still want to choose me after all the mistakes and failures that I have had. And I have even messed up after I gave my life to Him, but He continues to love me and to be with me.

John 3:16, "For God so loved the world that He gave His only begotten Son, that whoever believes in Him should not perish but have everlasting life."

John 15:16, "You did not choose Me, but I chose you."

Ephesians 1:4, "Just as He chose us in Him before the foundation of the world."

1 John 1:7-10, "But if we walk in the light as He is in the light, we have fellowship with one another, and the blood of Jesus Christ His Son cleanses us from all sin. If we say we have no sin, we deceive ourselves, and the truth is not in us. If we confess our sins, He is faithful and just to forgive us our sins and to cleanse us from all unrighteousness. If we say that we have not sinned, we make Him a liar, and His word is not in us."

God our Father created us in His own image, knowing

full well that we would mess up and be separated from Him by sin. But that didn't stop Him. And He was willing to give part of Himself, His one and only Son, as a ransom so that we could be purchased back out of slavery and bondage. That is the price He was and is willing to pay for you and for me. This is the most extravagant love that has ever or will ever be seen or known.

1 John 4:8, "...for God is love."

He is amazing. His love is unfailing. He longs to be with us. He longs for intimacy with us. He cannot stand the superficial relationship some try to pawn off to others that they say they have with Him. He wants to know us and for us to know Him and His heart, and His heart is full of love for us.

John 15:13, "Greater love has no one than this, than to lay down one's life for his friends."

Revelation 13:8, "...the Lamb slain from the foundation of the world."

True Christianity is all about relationship. Going through religious activities does not move the heart of God. This may come as a shocker to some, but your attendance record at church does not move God if it comes out of a wrong motive. It especially doesn't move Him if it is only on Sunday morning. In America this has become a sad ritual. Don't get me wrong, I am all for the local church, I have been serving in this capacity for eight years and it is very fruitful. But if your attendance is out of some haughty motive or a religious tradition, it is in vain. But my heart for worship comes from this love I have received from Him. Worship is one of our most fruitful and paramount things that we can do for our God. It is where we connect personally with Him. When we learn to praise Him and to worship from our heart unhindered, we actually enthrone Him. Our worship creates an atmosphere that invites Him and actually causes Him to come and inhabit the worship.

Psalm 22:3, "But thou art holy, O thou that inhabitest the praises of Israel."

So our worship is most important. It is the place we can create that the Lord will come and inhabit. If we are in need of God or His voice, or His touch, we have to create an atmosphere that is inviting to Him, and we do this through our worship. When you worship the Lord in total unhindered adoration you get to go to a place that not everyone goes in God. So many people are bound up by fear or worry about what someone else will or would say if they did step out in crazy praise or in total surrender. God is looking for the people who do not care what others say or might say. He is looking for the people who have a heart after His own heart. And when we have a heart after His heart, we will long for the times where we can get lost in His presence. We will long for the times where He will manifest His love and glory to us. Because it is in those times when He reveals to us personally who He is and how He feels about us. In worship is where true intimacy begins. We see the heart of God when we completely surrender to Him in worship. It is the place of connection.

Some of the most powerful encounters I have ever had have been in times of worship. Don't get me wrong, we have to have the word and pray, but worship is where He makes the truth of His Word come alive to us. When we lift Him up, He comes and inhabits our praise. Our worship is how we draw near to him so that He will draw near to us.

James 4:8, "Draw near to God and He will draw near to you."

I have learned to become a worshipper. There was a time when I was scared to even lift my hands in surrender. But God began to free me up. It was years, but I was becoming more and more hungry and passionate. When the Fire of God touches you, you can no longer be complacent. And when God touches you time and time again, that fire will increase more and more.

Once I was struggling and not feeling like worshipping or even much like doing anything. But there was a meeting our church put on for the men and I attended anyway. There was a man there who had never met me before. He didn't know that I had been a pretty radical worshipper. This was a point in my life where the enemy was trying to take my worship and my joy away from me because even the dinky demons know that if you are a *Praiser* you will always be able to get back to God, no matter what. So they targeted me and tried to steal my praise. But the man was a worshipper and while he was worshipping happily, the Lord spoke to Him about me. So he came to me and told me what the Lord had said. He said that for me to break through the attack and reconnect with God, He wanted me to lose myself in worship. God wanted me to go back to the place I was at and to even go on further than I had ever been with Him in my worship.

The man was so right. I began to get back into wholehearted worship and praise, even more and more than I had ever given to the Lord. And I am telling you that God began to touch me afresh. He began to soften my heart again, and He even increased the anointing on my life. My breakthrough out of lethargy came through me giving more in my worship. God increased the anointing on my life through my worship! People always say they want to walk in the power of God. If you really want to walk in the power of God, then go ahead and begin to worship Him like you have never worshipped Him before. Worship is your time to show Him you love Him. It is your time to show Him you appreciate Him. I love to worship and it blesses my heart to see others truly enter in. Lots of people never really learn to or even ever see someone truly get lost in worship. It is a powerful thing.

When I watch the young people I minister to truly connect with God in worship, it impacts me tremendously. If it does that much for me I can only imagine what it does to Father. When we lift Him up He sends His glory down. It does not matter what you do in worship as long as it doesn't take the focus off of God. If you become a distraction you will hinder what God wants to do. If you are like me and love to run and jump and dance and shout, I can assure you there will be some places and services that you will just have to stand still and connect softly and quietly so that you won't distract the complacent around you. Any way you worship is fine, whether loudly or quietly. The only thing that matters is your heart. If your heart is truly in your worship you will attract God and give Him a place to inhabit and make His glory known. And you can count on God, if you make room for Him, He will show up and touch and change your life.

I would encourage and do encourage everyone to step out of their own comfort zones and to press in to God with everything that they have within them. You will not be disappointed. God will not be outdone; the more you give the more He will give. He will not be indebted to anyone. Please try Him and see.

Just by praising and worshipping Him, I have seen Him come and change lives. Most people that truly love Him never want those times of worship to end. Once a person learns to connect with Him in this intimate way, it becomes a vital part of their Christian life. I have learned this and it has changed my life.

We have to understand that His presence is life itself. One moment in His manifest presence has the potential to completely change your life. One moment in His manifest presence can break depression, addiction, low self-esteem, wrong thinking patterns, and sinful habits.

Moses shows us that His presence is life sustaining in Exodus 24:18, and 34:28.

Exodus 24:18, "So Moses went into the midst of the cloud and went up into the mountain. And Moses was on the mountain forty days and forty nights."

Exodus 34:28, "So he was there with the LORD forty days and forty nights; he neither ate bread nor drank water."

Moses shows us that in the manifest presence of God your life can be sustained. Moses didn't eat or drink for forty days and forty nights and He didn't die! That is how powerful and life giving our God's presence is. So when His word says that He inhabits our praise we do not need to take it lightly. We need to begin to act on it and worship like there is no tomorrow.

There was a time in 2009 that I got very sick. I had a very bad cellulitis infection in my leg. I have had this happen many times, but this was by far the worst infection I have ever had. I had had the flu just prior, and my doctor told me this had weakened my immune system.

The infection lasted over three months. I was in a lot of pain and was hospitalized three different times, some of those hospitalizations were for a week at the time, and one was actually over a week. It was so bad I had to have a pick-line run into my vein directly to my artery above my heart for prolonged intravenous antibiotics. That was a new one on me. I had to take antibiotics twice a day through the line. I learned to tap myself and the medicine was portable, it was really amazing.

What I learned during this time was that my worship was my choice until I was sick. Being stuck in the hospital and being in so much pain, along with pain medicine, I was not able to worship some of those days at all. The Lord dropped a phrase in my Spirit during the first Friday night that I was unable to go to our teen ministry that I hadn't missed a Friday at yet. When I was in the hospital bed and the clock got to the time the ministry was to begin, I felt like I heard, "worship while you can."

The Lord was further showing me the importance of my worship. Worship is our privilege, not our duty. We need to make the most of the worship services and time we create for ourselves. It is vital and necessary.

He also showed me that He is so multifaceted that He never has to reproduce Himself. He is always able to show us something new about Himself. Even the angels who fly around His throne cannot go by another time without saying Holy, Holy, Holy. They have been flying around Him since creation, and they have not gotten used to Him or bored with Him yet!

Isaiah 6:2, "Above it stood seraphim; each one had six wings: with two he covered his face, with two he covered his feet, and with two he flew. And one cried to another and said: 'Holy, holy, holy is the LORD of hosts; The whole earth is full of His glory!'"

God showed me that in times of worship He gives us what we need. And each day our needs are different. Every time we begin to worship He can and will show us something different about Himself. He will put into us the things we need for that time in our lives. But what we have to see is that if we miss a chance to worship Him there will never be another chance for us to receive what He has to offer us at that time. He never duplicates. He always has fresh revelation and a fresh touch for each of us. And the way we receive it from Him is by whole-hearted worship.

I told you that your worship is paramount! You better worship while you can! You never know the moment or the day when you may not be able to, and then you will wish you had.

Let's learn to worship every chance we get and receive as much as we can from the Lord. In times of worship we can connect with God in such a personal and intimate way that we need never take a worship service for granted. Each time of worship has the potential to change our life and views of our heavenly Father. Once you connect with God in worship and He manifests His presence to you, and on you, and in you, your view will change about the importance of a time of worship.

Some people say things like, "why do they just keep singing the same thing over and over," or "they sing too long." These statements always point out who is a worshipper and who is not. A true worshipper does not watch the clock but watches the heart of God. A true worshipper doesn't care how many times we magnify the name of Jesus. A true worshipper doesn't care how many times they sing hallelujah. A true worshipper isn't concerned with singing a set number of songs, but is only concerned about an encounter with the manifest presence of the True and Living God.

This generation is stepping into a new era of worship. They and I alike are tired of just going through some religious motions with no encounter. Our God is alive! Jesus has risen from the dead and is alive forever more! So in our times of worship we need to expect an encounter with Him and not settle for anything less!

Revelation 1:18, "I am He who lives, and was dead, and behold, I am alive forevermore. Amen."

We worship a God who is alive! Hallelujah! He allows us to come into His presence and have genuine relationship. He lavishes His love upon us as we glorify Him and lift Him up. Worship is our time to connect and to commune with the One True God. So let's change the way we see worship services. Not as something to get through so we can just hear the Word. No, we need to look forward to the Word, but let's worship the God of the Word and enthrone Him and encounter Him and His manifest glory every chance we get, and when it is time for the Word of God to be taught after we have had an encounter, we will have so much more revelation.

God the Holy Spirit is the author of the Bible, and when we are in the Author's presence we will understand His message and heart with perfect clarity.

2 Timothy 3:16, "All scripture is given by inspiration of God."

2 Peter 1:21, "...for prophecy never came by the will of man, but holy men of God spoke as they were moved by the Holy Spirit."

Strive to connect with God in worship, don't settle for anything less than encounter. His love is available and His touch is fresh and new each day, so do not give up, and do not be satisfied until you have had a glorious and fruitful communion with the Holy Spirit.

Lamentations 3:22-23, "Through the LORD's mercies we are not consumed, because His compassions fail not. They are new every morning; Great is Your faithfulness."

So to me, times of worship are some of the most powerful times we can and I have had in His presence. It is one of the greatest opportunities of fellowship and relationship that can be had with our LORD. Please do not take them for granted, but rather fully engage yourself into those times and try to get lost in Him; you will not regret the time you spend with Him.

Psalms 16:11, "You will show me the path of life; In Your presence is fullness of joy; At Your right hand are pleasures forevermore."

> *"In Your presence*
> *That's where I am strong*
> *In Your presence*
> *O LORD my God*
> *In Your presence*
> *That's where I belong*
> *Seeking Your face*
> *Touching Your grace*
> *In the cleft of the rock*
> *In Your presence O God!"*
>
> *(From "In Your Presence, O God"*
> *by Paul Wilbur)*

Chapter Ten

Breaking Out of Religion Into Relationship

I can remember one of the first messages that the LORD ever gave me to preach. It was entitled, "Religion or Relationship, Which One Have You Got?" This seemed like such a simple topic and truth, but the more I looked into it the more religion I see in so many places than actual relationship. There are many who have and understand true relationship with God. But in south Georgia, I have seen a lot of different traditions that have been handed down and have become vain religious activities, and have no power whatsoever.

Mark 7:6, "This people honors Me with their lips, but their heart is far from Me."

We are such creatures of habit that if we don't watch closely we will almost always get into a similar pattern of doing things. When we see something work we want to continue doing it the same way. But sometimes the good is the enemy of the best. If we really learn to stay in relationship with God and to be led by the Holy Spirit, we will have to continue to change and keep moving with Him so we do not get stuck in a rut of tradition. God is able and does quite often do new things.

Think about this: Every sixty seconds is a new minute, every sixty minutes is a new hour, every twenty four hours is a day, every seven days is a new week, every four weeks is a new month, every twelve months is a new year, every ten years is a new decade, every hundred years is a new century, and every thousand years is a new millennium. So we can see God is in the new and fresh business.

Each day the children of Israel were wandering around the desert, God provided fresh manna. I love that because Jesus is the bread of life. He is the bread that came down from heaven.

John 6:35, "And Jesus said to them, "I am the bread of life."

John 6:51, "I am the living bread which came down from heaven."

Isaiah 43:19, "Behold, I will do a new thing, now it shall spring forth."

Isaiah 65:17, "...for behold, I create new heavens and a new earth; And the former shall not be remembered or come to mind."

Jeremiah 31:31, "Behold, the days are coming, says the LORD, when I will make a new covenant with the house of Israel and with the house of Judah."

Ezekiel 36:26, "I will give you a new heart and put a new spirit within you; I will take the heart of stone out of your flesh and give you a heart of flesh."

Now one of Jesus' attributes is His immutability. He never changes. His character and person will never change, but His creative power is so great that He never has to duplicate Himself either. He does not change, but He is constantly doing new things. His view of sin and rebellion will never change. His heart of love towards us is forever unchanging. But He is so full of creative power and life that He will always be birthing new ideas in His children. So get ready for some brand new things straight from the throne of Heaven that will completely line up with His written word.

Hebrews 13:8, "Jesus Christ is the same yesterday, today, and forever."

Though He never changes His character, He does have new things for us, and it should be easy to see that some things people did hundreds of years ago to reach the lost won't work today. The power and touch of God is still the same today and it will never change, but we have to be as creative as the enemy in packaging and distributing the love and power and message of Jesus. There are so many new things and advances in technology today that there are hundreds of new ways to get the good news of Jesus out there to people.

He has not changed. He is still full of love and grace and mercy. He is still a compassionate Savior who is moved by our weaknesses and our infirmities. He still offers us salvation through His death and resurrection. He still offers us healing by the stripes He took. He still offers us peace by the chastisement He took upon Himself. He still offers us relationship with Him by faith in Him and communion with His Holy Spirit. He has not changed, but the times have. Our message is still the same, man was separated from God by sin and Jesus came and paid the debt we owed and could not make payment on. He made a way where there was no way. And He offers us forgiveness of sins and everlasting life through faith in Him. But the ways we present this to people better change or else we will lose the next generation.

The statistics that were projected a few years ago showed a steady decrease in Bible believing Christians. From the baby boomers, which was around forty something percent, on down through generation X, which was around 16%, to the next generation with a projection of only 4% that would be Bible believing Christians. Well, that day has come and we are faced with a generation of only 5% that are Bible believing Christians. We have to see that the way the church has been doing things is not working and it is time for a change, in presentation only, not in the message at all. The gospel is good news and it is the power of God unto salvation. We don't have to add or subtract anything to it or from it. The message is perfect. And God has one thing about it that won't change: He chose the foolishness of preaching to present it and win the lost.

Romans 1:16, "For I am not ashamed of the gospel of Christ, for it is the power of God to salvation for everyone who believes."

1 Corinthians 1:21, "It pleased God by the foolishness of preaching to save them that believe."

I have seen the ministries that still do things the same way they did over fifty years ago. These ministries usually do not have any power in their services, and usually don't have many that are truly passionate about living for Jesus wholeheartedly. They are usually full of people who are just satisfied with doing what mom and dad did and keeping the same tradition alive. Most are not concerned about winning the lost or encountering God. They are satisfied with the status quo. I have even heard stories about some members of some churches wanting to have an outreach and give food away where other members who held a seat of power shut the plans for outreach down by saying that they did not want people to be coming off of the streets to their church. It is so sad to hear these stories where people are not interested in the things Jesus, Himself, was interested in, but only interested in doing things the way that they want them done, and to refrain from any change.

Religious services that are mapped out with no place or option for the Holy Spirit to move and minister are powerless and boring at best. They are not an accurate display of the love and power of Jesus Christ. He went about doing good and healing all who were oppressed of the devil.

Acts 10:38, "...how God anointed Jesus of Nazareth with the Holy Spirit and with power, who went about doing good and healing all who were oppressed by the devil, for God was with Him."

We need to learn to be led by the Holy Spirit. We must be sensitive to what He wants to do. He is God and He is here with us. We are supposed to work with Him and be in submission to His will. His will is good. He wants to bless us and to help us. He knows what we need before we ask so we have to learn to be led by Him and to stop trying to figure everything out on our own. God knows best. And when the Holy Spirit leads us and He uses us, the unbelievers will see this and know that we are in communion with the invisible God and that the message we are speaking is true.

Romans 8:14, "For as many as are led by the Spirit of God, these are sons of God."

Ephesians 1:9, "...having made known to us the mystery of His will, according to His good pleasure which He purposed in Himself."

Matthew 6:8, "For your Father knows the things you have need of before you ask Him."

1 Thessalonians 1:5, "For our gospel did not come to you in word only, but also in power, and in the Holy Spirit and in much assurance."

When we stop trying to please everyone else and begin to please only God, we will operate in power and in the Holy Spirit, and then will come much assurance.

In a good relationship there is real communication. That is where one person shares their heart and then allows the other to speak and share their heart also. Communication is only complete when both parties have spoken and listened. So in relationship with God, the Holy Spirit, we must not do all the talking, we have to be sensitive to His voice and His promptings. We also have God's written word that is vital to our relationship with Him. His word shows us His heart and His will. That is vital to our relationship.

So to have a healthy relationship with God we must have clear communication, read and become familiar with His word, and be willing to yield to the leading of the Holy Spirit.

We can see an amazing communication between God and man in Acts chapter 10. We can see this between a man named Cornelius and God, and between Peter and God. I want to take us through the text together and then bring out the points on relationship.

Acts 10: "There was a certain man in Caesarea called Cornelius, a centurion of what was called the Italian Regiment, a devout man and one who feared God with all his household, who gave alms generously to the people, and prayed to God always. About the ninth hour of the day he saw clearly in a vision an angel of God coming in and saying to him, 'Cornelius!' And when he observed him, he was afraid, and said, 'What is it, lord?' So he said to him, 'Your prayers and your alms have come up for a memorial before God. Now send men to Joppa, and send for Simon whose surname is Peter. He is lodging with Simon, a tanner, whose house is by the sea. He will tell you what you must do.'

"And when the angel who spoke to him had departed, Cornelius called two of his household servants and a devout soldier from among those who waited on him continually. So when he explained all these things to them, he sent them to Joppa.

"The next day, as they went on their journey and drew near the city, Peter went up on the housetop to pray, about the sixth hour. Then he became very hungry and wanted to eat; but while they made ready, he fell into a trance and saw heaven opened and an object like a great sheet bound at the four corners, descending to him and let down to the earth. In it were all kinds of four-footed animals of the earth, wild beasts, creeping things, and birds of the air. And a voice came to him, 'Rise, Peter; kill and eat.' But Peter said, 'Not so, Lord! For I have never eaten anything common or unclean.'

"And a voice spoke to him again the second time, 'What God has cleansed you must not call common.' This was done three times. And the object was taken up into heaven again.

"Now while Peter wondered within himself what this vision which he had seen meant, behold, the men who had been sent from Cornelius had made inquiry for Simon's house, and stood before the gate. And they called and asked whether Simon, whose surname was Peter, was lodging there.

"While Peter thought about the vision, the Spirit said to him, 'Behold, three men are seeking you. Arise therefore, go down and go with them, doubting nothing; for I have sent them.'

"Then Peter went down to the men who had been sent to him from Cornelius, and said, 'Yes, I am he whom you seek. For what reason have you come?' And they said, 'Cornelius the centurion, a just man, one who fears God and has a good reputation among all the nation of the Jews, was divinely instructed by a holy angel to summon you to his house, and to hear words from you.' Then he invited them in and lodged them.

"On the next day Peter went away with them, and some brethren from Joppa accompanied him. And the following day they entered Caesarea. Now Cornelius was waiting for them, and had called together his relatives and close friends. As Peter was coming in Cornelius met him and fell down at his feet and worshiped him. But Peter lifted him up, saying, 'Stand up; I myself am also a man.' And as he talked with him, he went in and found many who had come together. Then he said to them, 'You know how unlawful it is for a Jewish man to keep company with or go to one of another nation. But God has shown me that I should not call any man common or unclean. Therefore I came without objection as soon as I was sent for. I ask, then, for what reason have you sent for me?'

"So Cornelius said, 'Four days ago I was fasting until this hour; and at the ninth hour I prayed in my house, and behold, a man stood before me in bright clothing; and said, 'Cornelius, your prayer has been heard, and your alms are remembered in the sight of God. Send therefore to Joppa and call Simon here, whose surname is Peter. He is lodging in the house of Simon, a tanner, by the sea. When he comes, he will speak to you.' So I sent to you immediately, and you have done well to come. Now therefore, we are all present before

God, to hear all the things commanded you by God.'

"Then Peter opened his mouth and said: 'In truth I perceive that God shows no partiality. But in every nation whoever fears Him and works righteousness is accepted by Him. The word which God sent to the children of Israel, preaching peace through Jesus Christ—He is Lord of all—that word you know, which was proclaimed throughout all Judea, and began from Galilee after the baptism which John preached: how God anointed Jesus of Nazareth with the Holy Spirit and with power, who went about doing good and healing all who were oppressed by the devil, for God was with Him. And we are witnesses of all things which He did both in the land of the Jews and in Jerusalem, whom they killed by hanging on a tree. Him God raised up on the third day, and showed Him openly, not to all the people, but to witnesses chosen before by God, even to us who ate and drank with Him after He arose from the dead. And He commanded us to preach to the people, and to testify that it is He who was ordained by god to be Judge of the living and the dead. To Him all the prophets witness that, through His name, whoever believes in Him will receive remission of sins.'

"While Peter was still speaking these words, the Holy Spirit fell upon all those who heard the word. And those of the circumcision who believed were astonished, as many as came with Peter, because the gift of the Holy Spirit had been poured out on the Gentiles also. For they heard them speak with tongues and magnify God.

"Then Peter answered, 'Can anyone forbid water, that these should not be baptized who have received the Holy Spirit just as we have?' And he commanded them to be baptized in the name of the Lord. Then they asked him to stay a few days."

This whole chapter is amazing. In it we see God doing some new things and some things that totally went in opposition to the way things had been done for centuries.

When God gave Peter the heavenly vision it was in complete opposition with what Peter had been taught his entire life. Religion says this is the only way it can be done. But God the Father wants all to be saved and come to the knowledge of the truth.

1 Tim 2:3-4, "For this is good and acceptable in the sight of God our Savior, who desires all men to be saved and to come to the knowledge of the truth."

You see, Peter was not into religion but was in a real relationship. He set aside time to spend in the presence of God. And by doing so God was able to give him this amazing vision. Peter was in a trance and saw a vision or a video parable, a message in a vision. God also spoke to him and told him what to do. This is were we see the communion start, then Peter replies in disagreement. Disagreement is ok in relationship and communion, it is part of it. But Peter shows us trust and obedience when he yields to God's voice and command, even though he does not clearly understand what the Lord is trying to show him.

This is a beautiful picture of relationship. Sometimes we won't even understand what God is trying to teach us until we yield to the unknown. The Father and Peter were in communion but Peter still didn't understand. He was about to understand though because he was willing to yield to the voice of the Lord rather than wait until he could make sense of it all.

Everything Peter knew and had obeyed his whole life was being challenged at this time. He was going with Gentiles and going to enter their home. This was in opposition to the law but not to the voice of the Lord. Others went with him too. God's plan was to grant the Gentiles repentance unto life. But this plan had not been made known yet. So God was doing a new thing and using Peter to bring it to pass. You see, up until now there was no mingling with Jews and Gentiles, but God was changing things, and He uses us to bring the change. Only the ones of us who are in relationship will be sensitive to His voice and the leading of His Holy Spirit. The world will not be impacted and brought to Jesus because of our vain traditions, but only through our genuine relationship with Him.

Through Peter's yielding to the Holy Spirit the world was touched and continued to be changed. Because through this act of obedience the Gentiles received the Holy Spirit and the old way of ministering was changed forever. This rocked the religious crowd and they voiced their opposition directly at Peter.

Acts 11:1-3, "Now the apostles and brethren who were in Judea heard that the Gentiles had also received the word of God. And when Peter came up to Jerusalem, those of the circumcision contended with him, saying, 'You went in to uncircumcised men and ate with them!'"

They were unhappy, to say the least, that Peter had done something against the law. But we really can't blame them for they were truly zealous for God. But this should show us before we go popping off on someone for doing things differently from what we are used to that we should look to see God in it before we condemn them or their actions.

So Peter explained what happened in a great way and they saw that God was in it and rejoiced.

Acts 11:18, "Then God has also granted to the Gentiles repentance unto life."

I really like what Peter said in defense of obeying God and I still use this scripture to this day. This is what he said right after he told them about the Holy Spirit falling on the Gentiles.

Acts 11:15-17, "And as I began to speak, the Holy Spirit fell upon them, as upon us at the beginning. Then I remembered the word of the Lord, how He said, 'John truly baptized with water, but you shall be baptized with the Holy Spirit.' If therefore God gave them the same gift as He gave us when we believed on the Lord Jesus Christ, who was I that I could withstand God?"

Amen, Peter! Who are we that we should withstand God? That is a valid question.

Another text where God reveals the huge difference between religion and relationship is in the book of John. Let's look into it.

John 5:2-11, "Now there is in Jerusalem by the Sheep Gate a pool, which is called in Hebrew, Bethesda, having five porches. In these lay a great multitude of sick people, blind, lame, paralyzed, waiting for the moving of the water. For an angel went down at a certain time into the pool and stirred up the water; then whoever stepped in first, after the stirring of the water, was made well of whatever disease he had. Now a certain man was there who had an infirmity thirty-eight years. When Jesus saw him lying there, and knew that he already had been in that condition a long time, He said to him, 'Do you want to be made well?' The sick man answered Him, 'Sir, I have no man to put me into the pool when the water is stirred up; but while I am coming, another steps down before me.' Jesus said to him, 'Rise, take up your bed and walk.' And immediately the man was made well, took up his bed, and walked. And that day was the Sabbath. The Jews therefore said to him who was cured, 'It is the Sabbath; it is not lawful for you to carry your bed.' He answered them, 'He who made me well said to me, 'Take up your bed and walk.'

I love this passage. Here we can see so much. Jesus shows us that God is in the healing business. And I like to see this type of thing happening in the Bible where God was providing healing even before Jesus made the atonement.

There was actually a pool of healing, sounds like a fountain of youth, where God was reaching out to His people. Jesus asked this man a question but he must have been a crippled politician because he danced all around a simple yes or no answer. He replied that he had no man to put him in the healing water before someone else got in. So Jesus cut through the red tape of his answer and saw that the man did in fact want to be healed. And even though it was the Sabbath, Jesus was going to heal.

When Jesus commanded the man to rise, He also told him to take up his bed and walk. This command was in total opposition to the law of the day. But isn't it funny Jesus told him to do it anyway.

This man who had been obviously so sick that he could not even get himself up and into a pool of water for thirty-eight years was not interested in powerless religious activities. He was interested in getting healed and back to his life.

When Jesus performed the miracle healing in the man's life, the next command to take up the bed and walk may have been in opposition to the culture and law but he was more than willing to obey the man who obviously was in communion with God the Father. The man no longer cared to hear about vain and repetitious religious activities that could not get him healed. He was touched and healed by Jesus so now whatever He said the man was more than happy to do.

The Jewish leaders could not fathom why this man was breaking their tradition, but the man could care less. He had encountered Jesus and the raw healing power of God Almighty and whatever He said the man was willing to do. He quickly saw the powerlessness of men's commands and saw the power of God.

Therein lies the importance of yielding to the Holy Spirit of God. He is the Spirit of Truth. And we can see that God's character does not change but the way things used to be done has changed. And Jesus Himself brought the change. He shows us that the touch of God does not come from meticulously keeping vain traditions, but by living a holy life in relationship with the Father and the Holy Spirit. This is the only way to be connected to the power of God for healing and deliverance and everything else God has available for us. This power does not come through lighting candles or performing rituals but only through genuine relationship with God.

So you see, we don't please God just because we get up

and go to a church building on Sundays, or whatever days you go. We can only please Him by being in relationship with Him. This is not a couple of times a week thing, but it is a 24/7 thing. He is with us always. We need to strive to stay in communion with Him. Religion and activities will not set you or your family and friends free from their bondages or addictions. Our traditions and "same old—same old" routine won't heal the sick or deliver the oppressed. It takes men and women who are willing to pay the price and stay in communion with God. It takes individuals who will do whatever it takes to hear the voice of the LORD and obey it to break the power of the enemy and to shake cities for God. Jesus didn't die for religion, He died for relationship. So don't live for religion, live for relationship.

A point I preach very often about relationship is just being in His presence. Sometimes we don't even need words, we just need to be together. The Bible talks about deep calling out unto deep. (Psalms 42:7, "Deep calls unto deep at the noise of Your waterfalls; All Your waves and billows have gone over me.) In 1 Corinthians chapter 2 it speaks about the spirit of a man and the Spirit of God. It says that the Spirit searches the deep things of God. And the spirit of a man knows the things of man better than we know ourselves. So it seems to be a good thing to get in the presence of God and to let our spirit commune with the Holy Spirit, and we will actually receive revelation this way, even without saying a word.

This is an amazing aspect of Spiritual relationship. This is actually the deepest form of intimacy, our spirit in communion with God, the Holy Spirit. This is where God imparts to us His heart and desires. This communion is where we receive compassion from The Father and the desires of His heart become ours.

1 Corinthians 2:10-12, "But God has revealed them to us through His Spirit. For the Spirit searches all things, yes, the deep things of God. For what man knows the things of a man except the spirit of the man which is in him? Even so no one

knows the things of God except the Spirit of God. Now we have received, not the spirit of the world, but the Spirit who is from God, that we might know the things that have been freely given to us by God."

So sometimes things that are done in the Spirit look like they are not fruitful, but they in fact are. In the natural, if I stay in my office most of the day in the presence of God, in communion with Him, and just meditating on His word, it looks very unfruitful, when in actual fact this is one of the most fruitful activities we can do. To waste our life in His presence is very fruitful. Don't use this as an excuse to stop cleaning house all together, but some days it can wait. Our time spent with Him is not a lost investment. It is well invested. For later when you are in a place of ministry or prayer, then you will have a greater anointing on you and you will get to see the power of God in action. Only the people who learn true relationship will walk in the Holy Spirit and power.

Time in His presence is the most valuable aspect of relationship with Him. This counts reading the Word and prayer, but also includes meditation on His word and the silence of deep fellowship and communion. It is very fruitful.

Moses actually was face to face with God. Or those words could synonymously be said, presence-to-presence. That is both parties manifest together. I know God is omnipresent, but I'm talking about His manifest presence. When He makes His glory known.

Exodus 33:9, "And it came to pass, when Moses entered the tabernacle, that the pillar of cloud descended and stood at the door of the tabernacle, and the LORD talked with Moses."

Exodus 33:11, "So the LORD spoke to Moses face to face, as a man speaks to his friend."

Moses had the face-to-face encounter that I want. I hope that is what we all want. We need to strive to never be satisfied with anything less than true encounter. We must never be satisfied with anything less than real relationship.

What Moses had was and still is fruitful to this day. "Sometimes passion doesn't make sense." But time spent either in the quiet or in wild, loud worship with the LORD is very fruitful.

"For many are called, but few are chosen."
(Matthew 22:14)

Chapter Eleven

New Direction for the Call: A Call to the Hot House

That passion and desire to do more for God was still burning in me, even after years of youth ministry. We were finally able to have our youth meetings on the same night that the church had our usual meetings, on Tuesday nights. This helped a lot. We were in unity now. And it gave my wife and I a break from having to go another night more than the rest of our people, but not for long.

God was putting more of His desires in my heart to reach out to more young people, and just people in general. I know I have a call of God on my life as an evangelist to the teenagers and to adults as well. I love the children, but I usually get too "real" for the very young.

When the Spirit of God is upon you will be very bold. God started to give me more and more desires to reach this generation. Even though our church was so far out, scores of teenagers were getting to visit. They were coming from other churches and getting saved, and touched, and then they were going back to their churches. That didn't hurt my feelings that they weren't staying at our church for I was truly glad to get the opportunity to get them filled with the fire of God and send them back to their churches.

But I was yearning from my spirit to reach more and to see God touch more. I didn't know what to do but to pray and continue to go to their schools and love on them and just keep preaching to whoever came. I poured out my heart and imparted regularly.

My whole heart was to see them walk in the power and relationship that I had. I was not, and still do not, try to act as though I have this unattainable relationship with God. I want everyone to know that He is no respecter of persons and that anyone can be as close to God as anyone in the Bible. He just longs to be with us and He is not picky. I feel sometimes He is lonely because so many people think that they can't be close to Him because of condemnation. But there is no condemnation coming from Jesus at all.

Romans 8:1, "There is therefore now no condemnation to them which are in Christ Jesus, who walk not after the flesh, but after the Spirit."

Jesus did not condemn even the woman caught in adultery who was guilty of sin. He does not condone sin, but he does not condemn us. He loves us and wants us to come out of our sinful lives and start really living in Him, but He loves us to the Father. He does not try to condemn us to Him. It is the Holy Spirit's job to convict us of our sin, but there is a huge difference in conviction and condemnation. To convict us is to show us that we need to make a change, and that there is another way to go. So conviction causes us to turn from sin back to our Father.

Condemnation just beats us down and leaves us with no hope of our relationship with our Father ever being restored. Condemnation leaves us feeling abandoned and outcast from our Father. But we are not outcast from Him. He has done all He can to bring us back to Him. He has paid for all of our sin with His most precious possession, His only begotten Son, Jesus Christ. He paid for our sin with the blood of His One and Only Son. He loves us that much that He would pay the debt we couldn't possibly afford to pay with His Son. That is not condemnation but is love, and that is why we love Him because He first loved us.

1 John 4:19, "We love Him because He first loved us."

PROPHECY FROM THE LORD:

"I love YOU so much I don't ever want us to be apart;
I gave My Son, He is my very heart;
I gave Him for each one of you;
Yes, I gave My Son for each one of YOU."

So as this heart of God is stirring in me, I was becoming hungrier to minister and reach this generation in our community. By this time now I had been ministering in several different schools, prisons, and rehabilitation centers, as well as churches. I was discipling several young men. They were going with me to the prisons and schools and churches as often as they could. God was preparing a sold-out group of young men that would be willing to charge hell with a water pistol!

I watched them grow and the same hunger that was welling up on the inside of me was welling up in them too.

So after five years of ministry, I was in much prayer about the desires that were in my heart. I can remember the day the LORD began to give me the direction for the next season of my life and for the life of the fiery young men who were with me.

I was blessed with work at a farm near my house. My cousin was the foremen at the time, so he would offer me work whenever I had time to go. This was a blessing to me. The farm was one thousand acres. This place is huge. I love to go out there because it is so amazing to be away from everything and just to get on a tractor and pray and worship with nearly no distractions.

So this particular season and day we were bailing hay. So I was just driving around fields in circles all day raking the hay before the others came behind me with the bailers to bail it up. My job was very easy. So the entire day and for the weeks I worked out there, I would just pray and talk to God all day long. It was great to get paid to accomplish something and to pray all day.

So this one day, as I was praying for the community and for God to use me to do something big for His glory, He began to speak to me and give me divine instruction for our community. I heard the voice of the Lord say, "Go to McRae, get a building downtown, have church every Friday night, this is how you win the city."

I was blown away. I broke down and started crying like crazy and began to thank the Lord for speaking to me and allowing me to hear so clearly. I was overwhelmed and praised God. Those words rang out in my heart. I couldn't get them out of my spirit for anything. I knew this was the direction I had been praying about for years.

When God spoke those words to me, I could see exactly what He was talking about, and I knew this was going to be big. I called my team and got with them and began to share the vision of God with them and with some others. I should have paid more attention to Joseph. I only had a couple of people really say anything that was discouraging to my face. God told me to have church every Friday night so that is what I was going to do.

When I began to tell the plan of God, one man asked me what I was going to do about football season, because they have football games on Friday nights too. I said, "I'm going to do what God told me to do."

When I shared this vision with another man who was a friend of mine, he didn't say much at the time. And when I told him I was looking for a building, he just looked like he was in deep thought. The next thing I knew he was talking about trying to get a building and do something like I had shared with him. He was trying to beat me to what God had called me to. Those things hurt me, but I didn't let them detour me from the voice and the command of God.

When God said this to me it was not a suggestion, it was a mandate. He gave me direction to win a city! He told me to "Go to McRae", not think about where to go. He said, "Get a building downtown." Not if you would like to get one you might think about it. He told me to "Have church every Friday night", not some Friday nights.

So I took His word to me very seriously. And I knew it

would be a huge sacrifice for my family and me. But our sacrifice was nothing in comparison with the sacrifice of God for us.

We began to get our ministry incorporated. We wanted to have everything in order like we had never had before. In just a couple of weeks after the Lord spoke to me, we had our ministry incorporated. It is called Flamethrower Ministries, Inc.

Our student ministry at my church was already called the Flamethrowers because we wanted to light a fire for Jesus in others everywhere we went. So I felt this was to be the name of our ministry too. We love to get in the presence of God and we love His fire! God says He wants us hot, if we are cold He doesn't like that, or if we are lukewarm. Our temperature can make him sick if we aren't on fire for Him.

Revelation 3:16, "So then, because you are lukewarm, and neither cold nor hot, I will vomit you out of My mouth."

Sounds like if we are not on fire for Him it makes Him sick. I want to stay fiery for Him my whole life. He hates lethargy and complacency. So we should hate what He hates too. If we are alive we should have a high temperature. Only the dead are cold. That is one of the first evidences that death has set in a body; that the temperature of the body becomes cold. Yes, that goes for the church body as well.

So after we incorporated, we began to work on getting our 501(c)(3) so that we could receive donations and give the people a tax credit just like most every church in America. Keep in mind at this time not even one of us, my partners or me, were even thirty years old. This seemed like a huge step and it was. But we were going to do everything right because we didn't want to hinder the word and plan of God for our community and us.

After several months of working hard and raising money to cover the cost of all the paper work, we had everything done and sent off to the IRS. Once they have your paperwork there isn't anything to do but wait for them to process it. But we could pray and that always helps!

While all this was in the process, we were just about to explode to do something in this community with and for God. So we prayed and found an amphitheater in a local park and we scheduled two meetings. We booked a band and had dramas and preaching, and we saw some saved and healed in the two meetings. And to show you how God works, right after we stepped out in faith into a place we had never been before, God showed up.

The very next business day, Monday, when I checked the mail, we had received our 501(c)(3) status from the IRS! God provided after we stepped out in faith. And within five weeks of receiving our tax-exempt status we had found a building and cleaned it up and painted it and we were having our first service! God provided a building that was part of an old video store right downtown in a very busy location with the only downtown parking lot! It was just what we needed. It was a thirty-two hundred square foot building with no walls. There was one room in the back, and at the time, it was full of porno videos. God has such a sense of humor. It didn't have any running water either, but it was just what we needed.

The building was so old that it actually had two old bathrooms in it and they were very small. The holes for the toilet plumbing had been filled with cement though. The reason it had two wasn't for men and ladies though; it was for whites and colored. This place is ancient, but it was just what we needed. I call it our hole-in-the-wall. I love it. It is a brick building with big storefront windows.

We painted the bricks outside black, high gloss black! And we trimmed the building out in red. The reason behind the color scheme was that we wanted the place to be as anti-religious as possible. We didn't want it to look like a normal church at all. Because I knew if looking like a church would bring teenagers in, then all our churches would be full of them already. So we wanted to attract them not detour them.

God provided friends of mine and so many others to help us out. We knocked out the little wall between the old bathrooms and cut the two doors in half and made a great concession stand out of it. We got rid of all the pornography and made our bathrooms out of that one big room. We built a wall and split the room in two and had our water and plumbing run in there.

All we had to remove was all of the old video shelves and clean the place up, really. We painted it black and red too. Later we let the teenagers come in and paint huge murals all over the walls, and now it has come to life.

When God told me to have church every Friday night I had a vision of what it was to look like. I knew we would have lots of flashing lights and loud live music. It was to be different. If what was normal was working, He wouldn't have had to call us out in the first place. This was to be the beginning of something like other places I have seen and been to, but not exactly like any other place or ministry on earth. The look would be familiar to other fruitful youth ministries, though, bright, colorful, loud and powerful.

Our ministry's main focus is encounter with God. We stand on the word and we give our all in worship, but we want encounter with God, the Holy Spirit, more than anything else. We realize that once a person has a real encounter with Jesus that their lives will never be the same. You can have a religious activity and leave just the same as when you came in, but when you have an encounter with the True and Living God, you will never be the same!

So less than one year after the Word of the LORD came to me, we were in the *HOT HOUSE*, a place were we go to stay on fire for God. We named it the *HOT HOUSE*. This name alone does not sound religious, and many of our young people have come through the doors not knowing what to expect, and end the night in tears, giving their lives to Jesus and praying to be set free from drug addictions! PRAISE GOD!

And God is so hilariously awesome. We started having services at the beginning of the school year, and shortly after, football season did start. So here came our first test, to see if we would be faithful with little or much.

On our third service, we brought in a band, the JJ Weeks Band, and they drew a good crowd. But they were booked on a football night, so we didn't know how many would actually come. Well, God showed up in power and changed everything. He actually made history for us. For the first time in Telfair County history, they moved the Friday night game to Thursday because of supposed bad weather! The game was on Thursday and all the teachers, players, cheerleaders and band members were off and able to come on the Friday service! We had about one hundred and fifty people show up, and had around fifteen saved, and the weather was beautiful on top of that! GO AHEAD JESUS!

One of the teachers that was able to come that night was a friend of mine who had been going through some tough things and he gave his life to Jesus that night! I was blessed to look him straight in the eyes as I asked the people to give their lives to Jesus. He raised his hand and looked right at me. We made eye contact and I was able to speak into his life. This man stands out to me in importance because within two weeks after that meeting where God rearranged history, that teacher's life ended on this earth, but was able to begin in Heaven with Jesus, his newfound Savior.

The HOT HOUSE has become a platform for so many young people to share their testimonies and for up and coming bands to get to minister. There have been hundreds saved and thousands have heard the message of the Gospel of Jesus Christ. We have seen scores baptized with the Holy Spirit. And scores miraculously healed and delivered. We have been in intercession for the city and the power of God has been imparted into so many that we are truly gaining ground on the Word of the Lord; "This is how you win the city."

We also train the young people how to witness and pray

for the sick. We go out quite often to the streets and nursing homes and pray for strangers and the sick or lame. God has shown up in power so many times we truly believe that with God all things are possible.

Matthew 19:26, "But Jesus looked at them and said to them, "With men this is impossible, but with God all things are possible."

Chapter Twelve

Testimonies of the Miraculous

John 14:12, "Most assuredly, I say to you, he who believes in Me, the works that I do he will do also; and greater works than these he will do, because I go to My Father."

After reading the Word of God for myself, I began to see clearly that Jesus was and still is a healing Savior. There is so much healing in the Gospels that for someone to ask if it is God's will to heal only tells me one thing, they have not been in the word. If they are in the word and still question God's will to heal it is usually from wrong teaching passed down from generation to generation. If we read the word for ourselves, it is plain to see that Jesus was a healer and that did not stop when He ascended; it perpetuated through the disciples and is still available today. All we have to do is step out in faith and stand on the word.

Acts 5:12-16 "And through the hands of the apostles many signs and wonders were done among the people. And they were all with one accord in Solomon's porch. Yet none of the rest dared join them, but the people esteemed them highly. And believers were increasingly added to the Lord, multitudes of both men and women, so that they brought the sick out into the streets and laid them on beds and couches, that at least the shadow of Peter passing by might fall on some of them. Also a multitude gathered from the surrounding cities to Jerusalem, bringing sick people and those who were tormented by unclean spirits, and they were all healed."

I want to share just some of the miraculous things that I have seen God do through me and some others affiliated with the ministry God has allowed me to have. I have seen even more than what I will share. I am just going to share what either has happened through my hands or the hands of the ones I have been allowed to disciple first hand.

My wife has a cousin who, as a child and young teenager, was suffering from seizures. He suffered with the seizures for several years. We prayed for him one day and we didn't hear anything from them for a while. The next time we heard from them they informed us our cousin hadn't had another seizure since we had prayed. At the time it had only been a few weeks. Now it has been over two years and he still hasn't had another seizure! GLORY TO GOD!

Another of my wife's relatives had what appeared to be a stroke and collapsed at work. In the fall he also hit his head. He was in poor physical health before hand all ready. The fall put him in a comma. They placed him in ICU and called the family in because death seemed immanent to the doctor. They told the family if he did live he would have permanent brain damage. The family came and filled the waiting room. My wife and I began to share the scriptures about God's healing power with our family and our uncle's sons. They were only allowing two people at the time to go in and visit so all the closest family went in first. My wife and I waited to be last as the rest paid their last respects and told Uncle J.B. they loved him with no response because of his comma.

I used to carry a small bottle of anointing oil and use it in prayer. When our turn came to go in and pray, my wife asked me to anoint him with the oil. I had left the oil at home. So my wife told me to spit on my finger. I said no, I'm not going to put spit on him, he's in a comma. But as soon as I said no I heard the voice of the Lord say, "Spit on your finger." I said, "Ok, LORD."

So I spit on my finger. I didn't hock up a big one. I just kind of got that clear spit from under your tongue, but I did obey the voice of the LORD. Then I anointed his head with my spit and we prayed healing over him. We began to sing over him too. We just sang hallelujah. There was no response whatsoever. He was still unconscious and needed the ventilator to breath.

But the next morning, bright and early, we received the call from our family, Uncle J.B. was out of the comma and was totally coherent! No brain damage at all! He was out of the hospital in a matter of days, and is still alive now, over three years later! PRAISE GOD!

The next miracle that God used me for was amazing and it had more to do with Uncle J.B. This was actually about three days after he came out of his deathbed comma. GLORY TO GOD! I was waiting for a teenage friend of mine to take him to a school to lead worship and my son and I had stopped at a gas station to wait. I stopped by this particular station often because there is usually some men drinking beer and hanging out, and my friends and I usually pray for them and minister to them. It was no different this day. There was about five or more men sitting on buckets and old van seats or crates. Some had been drinking and some hadn't. I spoke to them for a minute and heard one tell me that he had had a stroke years ago and that one of his legs had been stricken with paralysis. I didn't even think to pray; I guess I was preoccupied with my son and our Frisbee. But when I sat back in my car, still waiting on my young friend, the Spirit of the Lord spoke to me and said, "When Rusty gets here, pray for the man." I jumped and said to myself, yea, I didn't even think about praying. Well, while I was sitting in my car, I saw my wife's uncle pulling into the store. I waved big at him and he came over to talk to me. He assured me he would be going to church this Sunday. He knew it was an absolute miracle that he was alive and now driving three days later. PRAISE GOD! I told him that sounded great, just go to church somewhere. He said he would be attending his home church he had grown up in. Then he went to hang out with the guy we were about to pray for. When my friend Rusty pulled up I said, "Hey man, let's pray for that guy over there." He quickly said sure, and we went to the man with Uncle J.B. sitting right there with all of the others. I asked him if we could pray for him and he happily agreed. This time I did have my oil and we anointed his head and leg and began to pray the prayer of faith. As soon as we stopped praying, I felt the gift of faith on me and I was sure he was going to be healed.

Before I could ask him anything, he looked up and said, "I feel better all ready." Then just like that he lifted the leg he said was paralyzed! When that leg moved his eyes and all our eyes got wide open. Then he looked at his friend and said, "Did you see that! I couldn't do that a minute ago!"

I said, "Do it again!" He did it again. I said, "Do it again!" He did it again! His leg was totally healed of the paralysis in an instant! I asked him how long it had been in that condition, he said, "For seven or eight years." God completely healed a man who had a stroke seven or eight years earlier in an instant.

Then J.B. spoke up and said to me, "Tom I might come to your church this Sunday." I told him to come on and then-kept shouting hallelujah!

In a youth meeting one night, a very tall young man came to me and said he didn't know how it happened but his collarbone was bent. It didn't look mirror image to the other. He said he hadn't hit it on anything but it was looking different and he didn't know why but he wanted prayer. I placed my fingers on his collarbone and began to pray. As I began praying, I felt the bone moving under my fingers. Then all of a sudden the Power of God hit him and he almost fell to the ground. He caught himself and stood up. He took me to a large closet and we looked at his collarbone with some of his friends, it was now the mirror image of the other. I didn't even know it but he had already shown it to his friends downstairs in the bathroom so they could tell it had moved and was looking like it was supposed to.

Then a young girl told us she had a vision while we were

praying and saw the devil drilling holes in his collarbone trying to break it down. But as soon as the enemy drilled those holes, God was filling them with Himself. That is when he almost fell under the Power of God. Then he said it felt like something was going on in his bone like it was being touched, and that's when the power hit him. PRAISE GOD!

Another one in my wife's family was amazing. There are several more in her family that are total, irrefutable miracles. I love to share them. This one had to do with Uncle J.B. again. This time it was his oldest son, Lee. He had been scheduled for a liver transplant already. They came to the family reunion and actually took up an offering for him because it was going to cost $10,000.00 out of his pocket for the operation. The pre-op was scheduled for the next day. So we had medical documentation that his liver was not functioning properly.

The family gathered around him and we began to pray. I led the prayer and then some other family members prayed while we were all in prayer. We anointed him with an aunt's oil and we reminded him of the miracle God had already done in his father's life. So we all prayed in faith, knowing that God had already done miracles in this family.

The next day he went in for the pre-op and the doctors told him his liver was working fine and they cancelled the transplant operation! He was totally healed! GLORY TO GOD!

Another of my wife's relatives, an aunt this time, was stricken with pain and blood clots. She had procedures done to try to help her. My in-laws asked me if I would go and pray for her, and I said, yes. I wasn't really in the know of how bad a shape she was in. She was in such bad shape that when she came to the door she was using a walker and had terrible bruising and swelling in both her legs. This aunt is not old enough to be using a walker. She began to tell us how many months of rehab and medicine she would have to have. She was in a tremendous amount of pain too. So I began to pray for her and she, too, is a Christian believer, so we joined our faith and stood on God's word.

At the time, she seemed to be the same, so we left. Sometime around 1:00AM that morning she called my father-in-law who had taken me to her house, which was her brother, and called, laughing out loud. She said that she was 100% better! She was totally healed and all the pain had left her legs and body! GLORY TO GOD!

One night at our church, on our regularly scheduled Tuesday night meeting, I was upstairs preaching to my teenagers and someone came up and interrupted us and told us to pray for a lady who had passed out downstairs. We stopped what we were doing and began to pray for her. She was a member of our church and I knew her well. The next thing we know another person came up and asked for my wife and I to come with her. She broke into tears and said she thought the lady had died. I told her surely she wasn't dead, but I was wrong. When my wife and I came around the corner, we saw Ms. Frankie Jean Carpenter lying on her back completely purple and surrounded by the entire church congregation in prayer and tears. Our pastor was at her head and was cheek-to-cheek in tears and prayer. There were three nurses on the scene taking her pulse, which was non-existent. Others were laying hands on her and in prayer. Still others were standing by crying.

I got right down with her and laid my hands on her left leg. I was in shock at first and I called myself going to give her an examination. So I actually picked her leg up and bent it to see if she really was dead. Keep in mind I have no medical anything, but I deduced that she in fact was dead, so then I really began to pray.

This was definitely a corporate effort, and we prayed for life. Within just a few minutes she began to cough. Life came back into her body and the nurses began to wipe her mouth out. This woman, who was undoubtedly deceased, was raised from the dead in front of forty plus witnesses right in the lobby of our church!

It turned out she was not feeling good, but got her mother to bring her to church anyway, and when she walked in the door she had a massive heart attack and dropped dead on her face. When an usher found her she screamed and the people came running and praying.

While she was dead, she later told us she had an out-of-body experience and she was able to tell us exactly who was laying hands on her. While this was happening, she was dead, but yet she told us, with vivid detail, what happened to her while dead. This is amazing! She actually heard the voice of her father, who had already passed away, tell her it wasn't her time and she had to go back. When she came back to life the ambulance arrived shortly after and took her to the hospital. She came back to church the following Sunday morning and said, "It's a beautiful day." GOD IS AMAZING! HE IS FULL OF RESURRECTION POWER!

One night in a youth center in Macon, Georgia, I was ministering and began to pray for the people. A young black lady came up that had hearing aids in both of her ears. I asked her what was going on. She had partial deafness in both ears, enough to need hearing aids, and she couldn't have been but in her mid-twenties at the most. I laid hands on her ears and prayed, and then I asked her to take them out and see how her hearing was. She took them out and put them in her pockets! When she left that night, they were still in her pockets! God restored her hearing! PRAISE GOD!

One day we had a few teenagers and young adults going out on the streets to pray for whoever we could find. We saw a group of people having a yard sale, so we pulled in to minister to them. It happened to be a church having a yard sale to raise money for their building fund. We asked if anyone needed any prayer and an older man in his seventies said he had bad gout pain. So we laid hands on him and cursed the pain and prayed for healing to come in Jesus' name. After we prayed we asked him how he felt.

He said, "Well, let an old man get up and see." He stood up and began to walk around and move his legs and knees and praise God. He said, "That feels a whole heap better!" PRAISE GOD, gout pain had to bow to the name of Jesus!

The same day we drove down the street to the local grocery store. When we pulled into the parking lot we saw a woman walking on a cane that looked like she was just dragging her leg. She was in terrible pain and you could see it very obviously. We didn't wait for the word on knowledge, common sense told us this lady needed prayer bad. My partner Joe was driving and we had three young ladies in the back seat of the truck, so I told the girls to go and pray for the woman.

Joe and I let them out and then pulled into a parking space and went to go pray for a man on a bench at the store. While we were praying for the man, we heard laughter in the parking lot. We knew God had healed and was pouring out His joy. We went to see what God had done and the woman was happily standing there on her own strength without the cane! She said all the pain had left her body and she was totally healed! The young girls told us that when they came up to the woman, she was in so much pain that she was actually rude to them. One of the teenage girls, Danielle, a mighty soul winner at age sixteen, asked her if they could pray for her and she said, "Ok, but make it quick, I'm in pain." I understand how she must have felt, but praise God, that there is a generation just crazy enough to believe God for the supernatural so that those in pain in parking lots can be healed and delivered from their pain! HALLELUJAH!

There were two different Friday nights at our youth center, the HOT HOUSE, where we saw people come in with leg braces on. One was a man and another was a lady. I asked in the middle of worship to pray for the man, and he agreed. Immediately after prayer, he took his knee brace off and put it under his arm. When he left it was in his hand, not on his leg! GLORY TO GOD!

The next week a woman had a knee brace on too, so I wanted to pray for her. I stopped the worship and called her out. It had to be God's timing because she was about to walk out the door. She must have brought a teenager and had worshipped some, and now was going to go on home. But I called out the mom who had a knee brace on, and she turned around and came back up front for prayer.

When she came up and lifted her hands, the power of God came upon her, and she began to cry and tremble, and we began to pray. It is amazing to see the faith in this family of teenagers who believe God for whatever needs someone may have. This woman went home and called back up later that night and told one of my leaders that she was not limping anymore! PRAISE GOD!

When my son was around three years old, I myself was beginning to get a fever, and my leg was starting to hurt very bad. He wanted me to get up and play with him in his room, but the pain was so bad I physically couldn't get up from my chair. I told him I couldn't get up because daddy was sick. Then I told him to pray for daddy. He laid his hand on my leg and said, "Name of Jesus, amen." Immediately the pain and fever left my leg and my body! I began to move my leg up and down and bend it back and forth, and then I started praising God! I told him daddy was healed and I jumped up out of my chair and went straight to his room and played with him on the floor for several hours. GOD IS GOOD!

Now my left leg has been an inch and a half shorter than my right since birth. I knew this and have prayed for my leg more times than I can number. But we began to see videos of legs growing out, shorter legs growing out, and lining up with the other. My faith started growing for this in my leg. I started to pray about it one week and watch many videos of others that this miracle was happening to. It was building my faith for it.

Well, one Friday night at the HOT HOUSE, I put on one of the videos for all the teens to see to build their faith. While it was playing the gift of faith hit me and I said, "Forget that junk, my legs got to grow right now! Come on let's pray."

I kicked off my shoes, sat down, and told everyone to come pray for me. They were amazed at how much shorter my leg was. I informed them I knew it was shorter but that it had to grow in Jesus' name. We all began to pray. All of a sudden, my femur bone in my left leg began to burn. It was on fire from my knee up about three inches. It was tremendously hot. I said, "Keep praying, my leg is on fire!" Then it started to happen, I felt something going on and I shouted, "It's growing, it's growing, it's doing it right now!"

My leg grew out a good inch longer while my feet were in my friend's hands! It was a total miracle! It was a creative, visible miracle in the hands of young faithful guys and girls. There was about seven of us praying and watching my leg grow out. I immediately jumped up and started to worship, and run around the HOT HOUSE! We praised God and shared that testimony that night, and that night we saw every person that came up for prayer healed and touched by God's mighty power! GLORY TO GOD!

One of the miracles that night, after I testified of my leg, was a fifteen-year-old boy who had hit a growth spurt and had grown several inches in the last couple of months. This sudden growth caused pain in his knees. His parents took him to the doctor and the doctor told him that his tendons hadn't grown when his legs grew. This left him in severe pain, and he couldn't even squat all the way down without being in terrible pain. He showed us how far he could squat down before we prayed. We laid hands on him and the power of God hit him. I asked him what was happening, and he said, "It feels like my tendons grew!" I laughed because I've never heard that before, but I guess he knows what that feels like now. I now know what it feels like for your leg bone to grow, so it really isn't too bizarre. He was totally healed! PRAISE GOD!

Another young lady had been in tremendous pain in her

kidneys. She had been diagnosed with a kidney infection. The pain had lasted for several weeks already. But when God began to heal others, her faith grew, and she came up for prayer. We prayed once, twice, and then three times. Each time she was getting a little bit better, but in the end of just a few prayers, all the pain left and she was totally healed. The next morning she sent me a text message and said she could finally get out of bed with no pain! I told her God was good. She said, "Yes, He is very good." GO GOD!

A nineteen year old girl had been in back pain for a long time, and unbeknownst to us, her leg was shorter than the other too. Her one leg was half an inch shorter than the other. She wasn't in pain at the time, but she suffered with chronic pain in her lower back most of the time. She sat down and another young friend of mine began to pray for her while many of us watched. Her leg instantly grew out, perfectly even with the other before our eyes! GLORY TO GOD!

There is another one of my wife's uncles who was diagnosed with cancer and had begun chemotherapy already. He had a cancerous growth in his neck that was visible. We went to his house one evening to pray for him. We took turns, my wife, his wife, my friend and I, and he himself praying against the cancer and growth. The cancerous tumor began to shrink while our fingers were on it. I could literally feel what felt like a pulse beat, and then it would go down in size a little more. When we were about to leave, Uncle Thad reached up and felt of the tumor and said, "It's about a third the size it was when you came." Praise God, a cancerous tumor was shrinking under the mighty hand of God! DO MORE LORD!

I have seen many different people's pain leave and immobility leave, and then mobility come in Jesus' name, but these are some of the standouts. God is touching me powerfully while I am rehearsing these stories. THANK YOU, JESUS.

In a high school in Jeff Davis County, I saw a girl in the gym that had an ankle brace on. I asked her if she was in pain and she said, yes, she was. So I asked her if God were to heal you right now, would you be able to tell? And she gave a resounding, yes! So I asked her if I could pray for her, and she said, yes. So I laid hands on the brace and I cursed the pain and immobility, and commanded healing and mobility to come in Jesus' name. I asked her how she felt and she was speechless! All she could do was laugh. She took the brace off and went on running around the gym, and when she left the class she left the brace too! GLORY TO GOD!

In the same high school, just a couple of weeks later, I was looking for another opportunity for God to heal. While a coach and I were walking through the halls, a girl came around the corner on crutches. That was all I needed to see! She stopped and was talking to the coach. I asked her what happened to her leg. She told me that she had hyper-extended her knee. She was a tennis player, which I didn't know at the time, but she was actually the number one ranked tennis player in her school. I asked her if I could pray for her and she said, yes. I laid hands on her and cursed the pain and immobility and commanded healing in Jesus' name. I also prayed for the Fire of God to come upon her and to be released into her knee.

After I prayed, I told her, "Your knee should feel hot and it should feel better." She said, "It is, it does!" We told her to move it around and see how it was feeling. She began to slowly bend it, and then she and the coach took off her knee brace and she put down her crutches and began to walk around the hall without them! Praise God! She said it was still a little stiff, so we prayed and thanked God for what He had done and asked Him to do more in Jesus' name. When we walked off, she walked away on her own strength, without the crutches. Her friend was playing with them and followed her. That was a Thursday and she was back in action playing tennis the next week! PRAISE GOD!

We prayed for a woman who had been suffering from acid reflux for weeks and weeks. She had been dealing with pain in her stomach for years, and it may have had something to do with the acid reflux, she wasn't sure. But she knew she was dealing with a bad case of acid reflux. It had already been diagnosed. We began to pray for her and the power of God came upon her. She could barely stand under the power of God. When we finished praying, she said it felt like something pushed the burning and pain down from her throat back down to her stomach! THAT'S GOD!

There was another night at the HOT HOUSE that was particularly astounding. There were more miracles in people's legs. A particular thirteen-year-old girl suffered with knee pain nearly every week. We would pray for her and the pain would leave, but every time the pain would come back. This night we thought to check her legs to see if they might be different lengths. Sure enough, her left leg was a good half-inch shorter than the right. The gift of faith was upon me, so I actually told about eighty people to gather around and to get ready to watch this girl's leg grow out. We even had the shorter ones up close to sit down so that the others that were gathered around could get a good view. God honored our prayers and our faith. The girl's leg grew right before our eyes in an instant! It slowly came right out, perfectly even with the other, and she has not complained with knee pain since! ALL GLORY TO GOD!

That same night there were four other people with legs that were shorter than the other. Most of them did not even know that they had shorter limbs. They had just been suffering with chronic pain so long it started to make sense, so we checked them out and saw what the problem was. One of them was one of my ministry partners. He had no idea one of his legs was shorter than the other. They prayed for him and his leg instantly grew out even with the other! Praise God!

Two of the other girls didn't know that their legs were shorter either, but when we checked them out, they were both visibly shorter. I wasn't even the one who prayed for them. I wanted the teenage girl whose leg had grown out a few weeks earlier to pray for them, and she did, and the legs grew out in front of over fifty witnesses! IT WAS TRULY AMAZING! PRAISE GOD!

One of the other girls knew her leg was shorter and it actually grew out a good inch. So many witnesses saw these miracles that they cannot be denied! But you guessed it, some people have tried to. God bless their little faithless hearts.

Everything Jesus did was SUPERNATURAL. So when He uses us, supernatural things will happen. We can do the natural things ourselves, but that is why we need Him and God, the Holy Spirit, to help us to accomplish the "supernatural." If you are a believer in Jesus, I cannot see why you would doubt that the miraculous still happens. God has done and is doing more than I have seen, but I am not about to stop seeking Him and all the miraculous signs and wonders He has in store for me!

One of my youth had received the swine flu vaccine and had gotten very sick. She was throwing up and getting dehydrated, so much so that she had to be put in the hospital. I received a text message telling me where she was, and I felt in my spirit that I needed to go and pray for her.

I got ready and went to the hospital. She and her mom were there, and they were glad to see me. The little girl, Jazzmine, said that she had had a dream that I came and prayed for her. I was so glad that I came. I had an appointment to meet with another of my youth, but I felt the urgency for me to go and pray with this one first. Then when she told me she had already dreamed that I came and prayed, it boosted my faith even more.

I hung out for a while. I laughed at her at first because she was under the influence of some medicine and she was very funny. I shared the scriptures on God's will to heal. (Psalms 103:1-5; Isaiah 53:4-5). Then I laid my hand on her head and began to pray. I commanded every spirit of infirmity to lose their grip and go in Jesus' name. When I did, she began to breathe very heavy, so I prayed some more. After the deliverance took place and the power of the enemy was broken, I looked to see how she was. She immediately sat up and said, "I want to get up and walk."

I said, "Go ahead." She got right up out of the hospital bed and grabbed her IV pole. I quickly unplugged it and hung it on the machine. Her mom looked shocked, so I just told her not to worry. She got right up and walked around her bed and right up to her mom, and stood smiling from ear to ear! I didn't know how bad a shape she had been in, so I asked her if she could walk before. Her mother said that she had been in bed for two days! She said that even when Jazzmine was in the wheel chair, that she had to hold her head up for her. The young girl couldn't go to the bathroom without her mom holding her head and helping her. But when the power of God hit her she sat right up and received her strength! She got out of her sick bed and walked under her own strength! It was amazing! I began to jump up and down right there in the hospital room and praise God.

It was an instant miracle. She completely sobered up from her medicine too. The young girl was overjoyed and could not stop smiling, and neither could I! I LOVE YOU, JESUS!

I was asked to speak at a GGFC (Guys & Girls for Christ) meeting at the Dodge County High School. I knew most of the teenagers, and so I began to share of all the miracles that I have been seeing God do recently. Most of the teens go to a denomination that does not preach about the healing power of God. But I had to share what the Lord had put on my heart, and I am so glad I did. I told the story of my leg growing out and the day I was preaching is the same day the girl was healed who had the ankle brace on. I had been to three different high schools that day. So I saw a miracle healing at the second, and now at the third, I was testifying of it.

When I finished sharing, one of the sixteen-year-old guys raised his hand with a question. I wasn't sure what he was about to say because I had just told him a lot of amazing things. He started out by saying, "So you're telling me that you prayed for your leg to grow and it grew. And you're telling me that you prayed for a girl's ankle today and it was healed."

I replied, "Yep, that's what I'm telling you." I didn't know where he was going with this, and I was hoping it wouldn't lead to an argument. Sometimes people will try to refute the touch of God and I didn't want this to be one of those times. And praise God, it wasn't!

He looked at me and said, "Well, I've got these flat feet." That is all I needed to hear.

I jumped off of the desk I was sitting on and said, "O, you got faith to pray!" Then he shared that his dream was to get into the Air Force, but he knew that they would not accept him if he had flat feet. I had shared enough about God's healing power that it had created faith, and he was ready to pray.

I went to him and he asked, "Do I need to take my shoes off?" I told him he could do whatever he wanted to do. So he took them off. This young boy named Conner, had the biggest, flattest feet I have ever seen. He is six-feet, four-inches tall. He's huge! So you can imagine how long his feet were.

I laid my hands on his feet right where the arches are supposed to be, and I started to pray. All the other teens and teachers came up to pray and watch. I had just shared for over an hour about all the miracles I had seen, so they were in faith wanting to see some too. I prayed for a minute, and I felt tingling in his feet. I asked him if he felt anything, but he had his head down on the desk. So I prayed Psalms 37:4 over him. The scripture says, "Delight yourself also in the LORD, and He shall give you the desires of your heart." I knew his desire was to get into the Air Force and that he loved Jesus.

This young man is an exceptional young man who had been leading worship earlier in the meeting. I knew he loved Jesus, so I could pray that over him. Then I looked up and asked him what was going on. He picked his leg up, while still sitting in his desk, and put his foot on the top of the desk. He is some kind of flexible.

He began to look at his feet intently. I asked him if there was an arch. He didn't say anything, so I leaned to the side where I could see the bottom of his foot myself. When I did, I could see light under his feet! They had been so flat and now they had high arches in them. God formed arches in Conner's feet while sitting in the classroom of the public high school! He began to shout as loud as he could, YES! YES! He began to cry tears of joy! He jumped up and gave me the biggest hug ever. He exclaimed, "MY MOM IS GONNA FREAK OUT!"

This young man's dream could now be attained because of the miracle working power of God! JESUS STILL HEALS TODAY!

Mark 10:27, "With men it is impossible, but not with God; for with God all things are possible."

Mark 9:23, "Jesus said to him, 'If you can believe, all things are possible to him who believes.'" GLORY TO GOD! GLORY TO GOD!

I got a lifelong friend of mine to help me take care of a few things one day, and while we were riding in my car, he told me that his shoulder was in a lot of pain. He said that his rotator cuff was messed up and the doctor was sending him to a specialist because he needed surgery on it. I told him we would pray for it and God was going to heal it. He didn't really pay me much attention, and he just kept on talking while we were riding. I was not joking when I said it, but he didn't have faith for it yet.

Then he showed me his middle finger on his right hand and said he had broken it, and was unable to bend the last knuckle. I told him the same thing, that we would pray for it and God would heal it. He kept on talking, not paying me much attention.

Still later, he mentioned he was having kidney problems

and high-blood pressure. My friend is only twenty-nine years old, way too young to be having all these problems. We talked a while and caught up, and then I began to share about what God was doing in my life and ministry, and I told him we would pray.

Before we prayed, I asked him to show me how much he could move his shoulder with the torn rotator cuff. He couldn't reach between his shoulder blades. Just to get close to touching his head caused him immense pain. He grimaced when his hand got close. He was nowhere near having full mobility.

Now he was ready to pray, so I laid my hands on his shoulder and began to rebuke the pain and immobility. As I did, the palm of my hand became hot. I could feel the healing virtue of Jesus Christ of Nazareth going through my hands into his shoulder.

I said, "Man, do you feel that heat?" He said he felt it. The presence and the power of God fell on us and I began to pray like a wild man. I forgot what else was wrong with him, so I asked him, and he reminded me about his kidneys. So I prayed for those kidneys and that high blood pressure. Then I went ahead and prayed for the Fire of God to fill him! When I did, he snatched off his hood, and it was a cool day.

Then he exclaimed, "Man, my legs are on fire!" The Fire of God came on him and he began to sweat!

He told me, "Man, I'm sweating!" This was a very cool day. We had on jackets and he was wearing a hood too. But when the Fire of God hit him, he threw that hood off and was still sweating!

Then I finished praying and told him to slap his back with the hand that couldn't reach before. He looked me straight in the eyes and began to lift that arm and shoulder up. It got closer and closer and then it went past where it had stopped earlier, and his eyes got bigger and bigger! He was totally healed and regained 100% full mobility back in that shoulder! All the pain left and he was in shock! He began to tell me how he couldn't do that earlier, and I told him, "I know, that's why I had you show me before we prayed so I could give God glory!" He was amazed, and I began to rejoice.

Then the Spirit of God hit me and I began to declare some things to him pertaining his life with God. And the Lord impressed upon my heart to declare that his body was healed, kidneys and blood pressure, according to Mark chapter 2.

In the text, Jesus saw the paralytic's faith and told him that his sins were forgiven. Then the Scribes, Pharisees, Sadducees— "Couldn't sees" and "Wouldn't sees" - put their two-cents in and said that He was blaspheming, so He proved Himself to them, that what He said in the invisible realm was happening just as real as in the visible realm.

Mark 2:3-12, "Then they came to Him, bringing a paralytic who was carried by four men. And when they could not come near Him because of the crowd, they uncovered the roof where He was. So when they had broken through, they let down the bed on which the paralytic was lying. When Jesus saw their faith, He said to the paralytic, 'Son, your sins are forgiven you.' And some of the scribes were sitting there and reasoning in their hearts. 'Why does this Man speak blasphemies like this? Who can forgive sins but God alone?' But immediately, when Jesus perceived in His spirit that they reasoned thus within themselves, He said to them, 'Why do you reason about these things in your hearts? Which is easier, to say to the paralytic, 'Your sins are forgiven you,' or to say, 'Arise, take up your bed and walk'? But that you may know that the Son of Man has power on earth to forgive sins' –He said to the paralytic, 'I say to you, arise, take up your bed, and go to your house.' Immediately he arose, took up the bed, and went out in the presence of them all, so that all were amazed and glorified God, saying, 'We never saw anything like this!'"

That text went through my mind and my spirit when I

saw my friend's shoulder healed, and then I declared to him about his blood pressure and kidneys. We couldn't see those miracles, but because of the one we could see, I fully believe he received the other two at the same time. And God showed us something else to build our faith even more. After we enjoyed God's presence and the Fire of God lifted, we walked outside to his porch. Then I remembered about his broken finger, so I asked him to check it out. He held out his hand and we looked at his fingers. Then he slowly made a fist, and the finger that he had not previously been able to bend, bent completely and had no more pain in it! PRAISE GOD! Things got healed that day that we hadn't even mentioned!

I'm telling you that when the healing power of Jesus Christ hits you and touches your life, you can be made whole! My friend's shoulder was completely made whole, along with the broken finger, and by faith his kidneys and blood pressure too! GLORY TO GOD IN THE HIGHEST!

There was a young girl who recently got saved at one of our meetings, and after the prayer of salvation, I called out prayer for anyone who had pain in their bodies. She came back up and said that she had a bone disease that caused her bones to be easily broken. She also said she had tumors in her body right then. We prayed and cursed the bone disease and the tumors, and instantly the tumor left from her spine! I told her in faith that the tumor was gone, and when she felt where it had been, it was no longer there.

I said to her, "It's not there, is it?" She couldn't even say a word, she just shook her head no in agreement that it wasn't there, and then she broke down into tears. GOD LOVES HIS CHILDREN! HE IS STILL COMPASSIONATE! GLORY TO GOD!

One night at dance practice, one of our women who had practiced, was wearing kneepads because of arthritic pain. I told her we could pray and curse that arthritis. She agreed. She came and sat beside me in our church seats. I shared Matthew 17:20 with her which says, "...for assuredly, I say to you, if you have faith as a mustard seed, you will say to this mountain, 'Move from here to there,' and it will move; and nothing will be impossible for you."

So we began to pray, and the moment I released the healing power of God to fill her, the Power of God hit her and she jolted up in her seat and almost fell out of it. Her friend was leaning over from the row of seats in front of her and she was laying hands on her too, and when the Power of God hit the one lady, it went through her and hit the other one too! They both shouted out loud.

Well, I just kept right on praying and the Power of God hit her two more times hard. After that, she got up with tears in both her and her friend's eyes, and got out of the row of chairs and started to take her kneepads off. She took them off and then she bent down on each knee and stood back up without pain and under her own strength! GOD DID IT AGAIN! PRAISE GOD!

The miraculous healings are not all I have seen God do, but they are amazing and great to build faith in nonbelievers, as well as believers. The most powerful miracle of all is when someone gives their life to Jesus. This is awesome, and I have seen it happen in some of the most unimaginable places.

One day I was at a school where I had attended an FCA (Fellowship of Christian Athletes) meeting. I am on staff and have volunteered with this ministry for many years. It is a way I can get into public schools and not only meet young people, but minister to them as well. After the meeting, I was in a classroom with a teacher who also was a youth minister at another church in our community. While in class talking to the students, an announcement came over the intercom, "Evacuate the building!" It was a bomb threat! The entire Middle school and High school had to be evacuated. I was in the middle school, so we went to the football field. The high school went to the baseball field.

When we got out there, I was able to talk to the entire

middle school. I went to a group of students that I knew and began to hang out. The Spirit of the Lord came on me all of a sudden and I began to ask one of the young men and was speaking loud enough for many others to hear me, if he were to die today was he 100% sure, without a shadow of a doubt, that he would go to heaven. He responded that he wasn't sure.

Well, I took him and the others through some scriptures out of the book of Romans. (Rom 3:23; 6:23; 10:9-10) Then I shared with them that if they wanted to give their lives to Jesus, they could pray with me and surrender to Him. I told them it wasn't about attendance in a church, but salvation is a relationship with Jesus. I prayed and then I asked who had prayed with me. When I looked up, three different students prayed with me and gave their lives to Jesus at a bomb threat evacuation! GLORY TO GOD! Take that, devil!

I have led people to the Lord in drive-through windows of fast food restaurants. I have led people to the Lord while they were working at convenient stores too. I have led hundreds of students to the Lord while in school, many during class time. Sometimes God opens the door for me to tell a funny story, and then He opens the door for the Gospel, and they respond with, yes, to Jesus!

We have seen people give their lives to Jesus in parking lots, nursing homes, in vehicles, classrooms, and parks, and yes, even in churches! There truly are no limits with God and His saving grace.

Hebrews 7:25, "Therefore He is able to save to the uttermost those who come to God through Him, since He always lives to make intercession for them."

I have some of the most amazing and faith-filled teenagers in my ministry, and they never cease to blow my mind. One young girl, Danielle, seems so shy, but she is a mighty one-on-one soul winner. She sometimes fasts lunch in her high school, and gets a couple of buddies, and they go from table to table witnessing to her entire school. She ends up with many giving their lives to Jesus.

One of her coolest testimonies to me was the time she told of another student wanting to copy her paper. She said the girl passed her a note and it read, "Can I copy your paper?"

She replied on the note, "No, if you were to die today, would you spend eternity in heaven?" Then she passed it back. The girl responded, no, and ended up giving her life to the Lord in class while passing notes! THAT IS THE HOLY SPIRIT IN ACTION! GO GOD!

The same young had a burden for the students on her bus too. One day God opened the door and she went through. She stood up and shared the message of Jesus to some very intimidating students. When she finished, nine out of ten gave their lives to Jesus! PRAISE GOD FOR BOLDNESS!

Acts 4:31, "And when they had prayed, the place where they were assembled together was shaken; and they were all filled with the Holy Spirit and they spoke the word of God with boldness."

That same young girl, Danielle, founded her own high school club, "The Freedom Dancers", and had it approved by the state of Georgia all by herself! She is always leading a few students to the Lord here and there; Jesus is always on her mind.

Our church gave away food one day in our community. I got the teenagers and some of my leaders ready to win souls. We had them lined up to get the food. They were waiting, so we went out to them and I showed them a good way to witness, and with six of us, we led fifty-eight people to the Lord in just a couple of hours. That same young girl, Danielle, led seventeen of the fifty-eight to the Lord that day.

One of my leaders went to pray for strangers in a grocery store one day. We were all out in teams, storming the city. He went up to a lady and began to witness to her and offered to pray with her. She told him she had been in an automobile accident, and was in pain, and had been ever since. He began to pray, and the healing power of God hit her and she broke out into tears. She then thanked him and he went on his way.

A couple of weeks later, my pastor received a letter from the woman wanting to thank my friend, Joe, for praying for her, and to let us know that all the pain had left her body and she was totally healed in Jesus' name! PRAISE GOD!

With all these miracles and the hundreds upon hundreds of salvations we have seen, we are going to continue to trust the Lord and believe Him for more of the supernatural.

I hope this has stirred up all who hear about God's love and power to step out in faith and see what He can do through you. It reminds me of another scripture.

Luke 9:1-2, "Then He called His twelve disciples together and gave them power and authority over all demons and to cure diseases. He sent them to preach the kingdom of God and to heal the sick."

Luke 9:6, "So they departed and went through the towns, preaching the gospel and healing everywhere."

That is still what Jesus wants us to be doing. We are to be preaching the gospel and healing everywhere!

Matthew 10:7-8, "And as you go, preach, saying, 'The kingdom of heaven is at hand.' Heal the sick, cleanse the lepers, raise the dead, cast out demons. Freely you have received, freely give."

I hope that we all pray for boldness and faith, and continue to work the works of God while we still have time. We are the light of the world, and if we don't shine, everyone will stumble around in darkness. Jesus commissions us to take up where He left off.

Matthew 28:18-20, "And Jesus came and spoke to them, saying, 'All authority has been given to Me in heaven and on earth. Go therefore and make disciples of all the nations, baptizing them in the name of the Father and of the Son and of the Holy Spirit, teaching them to observe all things that I have commanded you; and lo, I am with you always, even to the end of the age.'" Amen.

Mark 16:15-18, "And He said to them, 'Go into all the world and preach the gospel to every creature. He who believes and is baptized will be saved; but he who does not believe will be condemned. And these signs will follow those who believe: In My name they will cast out demons; they will speak with new tongues; they will take up serpents; and if they drink anything deadly, it will by no means hurt them; they will lay hands on the sick, and they will recover.'"

Mark 16:20, "And they went out and preached everywhere, the Lord working with them and confirming the word through the accompanying sings. Amen."

Chapter Twelve

Staying Strong Through Death

Now in the year 2009, my wife, Dell, and I were starting to feel the unction to enlarge our family. We had our son, Kaiser, in the first year of our marriage, and we did good to raise him and try to keep everything together. We had our hands full with the different ministries we were involved with. People always asked us when were we going to have another child. They started asking about the time we got to hold Kaiser right after his birth. The answer I gave them that always shut them down was, "Well, God only had one son and He turned out pretty good." End of discussion!

But at this point in our marriage, something shifted, and all of a sudden, we were ready to try to have another one. So we prayed together and told God we would do our part and it was ok with us for Him to give us one when we were ready.

It didn't seem like very long and the Lord granted to us our request! We found out that Dell was pregnant. It was so exciting. Not only was Dell pregnant, but also five other women in our church were pregnant too. One of our partners in our ministry and his wife were expecting as well. She was one of the five women that attend the same church as we do.

We had prayed and hoped that we could have a child around the same time as our ministry partners. They were newly weds, and we knew they would have one soon. So God answered our prayer, and Dell and Brittni, our ministry partner, were expecting at the same time. Our friend, Brittni, was about two months farther along than Dell. So God was blessing the fruit of everybody's womb!

We were so excited and we began to let everyone know, and we told Kaiser. He had wanted a sibling for some time now. Then we began to pick out names and dream about whether we were having a boy or a girl. This is always an exciting time. I am one of those who wants to know right now; I cannot stand to wait. Even when I talk to people, I want them to get to the point. Don't beat around the bush with me; just spit it out. But with this type of thing you just have to wait the four months until everything develops. There is no sure fire short cut unless the Lord just shows you. And a funny thing happened; the Lord did show a lady in our church.

This particular woman, Ms. Bonnie, is a great friend of ours and she is like another mother to us. She is in communion with the Lord like not many others. She is just in love with her Savior and stays in communion with Him in an amazing way. So when she said she knew what we were having, I asked what it was. She wouldn't tell me though. The Lord showed her what Brittni and Dell were having, but she wouldn't tell us.

Well, the day came and they found out that Rusty and Brittni were having a girl. When Ms. Bonnie's kids told her that they were having a girl, she told them— "I know she is having a girl, God already told me." But she wouldn't tell us what we were having yet.

Dell had been to the doctor and had a sonogram, and came home with a little picture of the baby. You could barely tell that it was a baby, but we have been here before so we knew that was the beginning of life and it was awesome!

I missed the first visit, and I didn't want to miss another one. I went to every visit with Dell while she was pregnant with Kaiser, and I was there at his birth and cut the cord myself. I like to be involved in my kid's lives. I can't stand to miss a thing.

So the next visit came and I picked up Dell and drove her to the doctor. We went to the back and then we went to the sonogram room. The lady was very nice, and we got ready to get to see this baby. Dell was only around two months along, so we still wouldn't be able to find out what we would be having, but at least we would get to see the little child.

The lady came in and got Dell ready, and she started to do the sonogram. All of a sudden, there it was, our little baby. I could see the baby easily. I could tell where the head was and the body, and even the little arms and legs. I was so excited! We looked for a few minutes and then Dell asked a question, "Shouldn't we be able to hear the baby's heartbeat?"

When I looked up at the woman, she had a shocked look on her face. I knew something was wrong. The lady said, "You should; I hate to have to tell you that."

The shock and fear hit us all of a sudden out of nowhere. I looked back at the computer and I could see now that the baby was on the screen, but the baby wasn't moving. My heart sank, and it is sinking again as I right this.

Dell began to cry, and the woman began to tell us that she was sorry, and she went to get the doctor. No one said it with words, but the message was loud and clear—the baby was not alive anymore. I immediately put my hands right where the sonogram machine had been taking the pictures of the baby. I began to declare life, and prayed against death for my child. As I was praying, Dell was crying, and then the doctor came into the room. He heard me praying, and when he came in, I told him to check it again. He said, "Ok, you prayed, we'll check it again." Then I called my pastor and I was so glad to know that he is a mighty man of God. He, himself, has seen four people raised from the dead. When I told him that they were telling us the baby was dead, he immediately went into prayer with me over the phone. He declared life, and I was in agreement with him. While he prayed, the lady came back in and began to look again. The baby looked the same and there was still no heartbeat. I was still in faith that this baby was going to live. We had been praying over all the pregnant women at church already, and I had personally prayed for our child with Dell and Kaiser many, many times in the short month we knew about the pregnancy.

When nothing had changed, the doctor told us to come back on a Friday to have a DNC, the procedure to remove the baby from the womb. When we left, we had the whole church in prayer for our baby to live, and we prayed in the Spirit all the way back from the doctor's office to our house, which is an hour-long drive. We cried and prayed the whole way home. I fasted and we prayed that night and we decided to go back the next day and have another sonogram done, believing God would raise our baby up, and that this baby would be another miracle testimony unto the Glory of God.

We arrived the next day in faith that our baby was alive and we were ready to see. We went back into the sonogram room with the lady. She was truly a sweet woman. She was very sympathetic, and it was genuine. She told us that she had never been able to have children at all. When we told her we did have one son, she pointed out the positive that we had already been blessed with more than she ever had.

This was true, we are so thankful for our son, Kaiser; we have a love for him like God has for each of us.

Now it was time to look again at our little baby and see if life had been restored. She gelled her belly up and began to look, but there was still no life. We had faith and we had to check again. If we hadn't done that we would have always had regrets. But we had checked again and there was no life. The reality started to hit me then. I had not been in denial, but I had been in faith, and I totally believed that we would get our resurrection miracle. We have already seen that resurrection power in action, so we know that aspect of God. This time we did not get the desire of our heart. And I will go ahead and end the discussion in people's minds; this was not the will of God for our baby not to be born."

John 10:10, "The thief does not come except to steal, and to kill, and to destroy. I have come that they may have life, and that they may have it more abundantly."

That baby is no doubt in heaven. But God wants us to have life and choose Him not to just take us. The Bible clearly shows us that the thief, Satan, our adversary, comes to steal, kill and destroy. God does not kill babies. Jesus came that we could have life, not death.

There was not even one split-second where we ever got mad at God or blamed Him for the tragically sad events that were taking place. He loves us so much that this was not only tearing our hearts to pieces, but also His. He feels more deeply than we do. The emotions we feel are only a fraction of what He feels. We are actually created in His image and likeness. (Genesis 1:26). We feel the same things He feels. That child was and is as much, if not more, His than ours. He hates to see us have to go through that and He went through it too. He gets absolutely no pleasure out of seeing His children hurting like this. No parent, in their right mind, would be happy about their own children suffering through something like this, and neither is God our Father.

And to end another incorrect ideology about why this happened, God does not kill off babies who might have physical or mental problems, people do, but God does not. Many in America are so greedy for money that they have devised an ungodly scheme. They want to do dangerous and costly procedures to check and see if a baby might have Down's syndrome or any other physical or mental defect. And if there is a slight possibility of some problem, offer them a costly abortion to line the doctor's pockets and discard the blessing of the Lord like some disposable diaper.

Sounds a lot like Hitler's plan to me for a super race of people; or like mere men are playing the role of God, the Father, themselves, to determine who can live or die. I praise God this wasn't the fad when my mom was pregnant with me, or I could have been one of these innocent casualties also.

But some people had the idea and audacity to tell Dell and I that God knows best, and that something might have been wrong with that baby, so that might be why He took the baby. That is totally wrong, and fifty years ago that thought pattern was unheard of. Now, with abortions so common, it seems as though the world and the culture of America, especially, has been desensitized to the innocent slaughter of millions. So we now have a warped view of God too. And if that was the case, why do we have anyone on the planet with birth defects or disabilities? God is not the cause, sin is. But children are a blessing from the Lord.

Psalms 127:3, "Behold, children are a heritage from the LORD. The fruit of the womb is a reward."

So I want to make it clear that I do not believe that God took our baby. He has our child now with Him, that's for sure, but He did not kill the child. The stinking, dirty devil and the sin he brought into the world, caused the loss. I do not have all the answers to life's questions, but Jesus is good, I know that. And He does not need our child or anyone else's child in Heaven, He has it all under control. Heaven is a reward and He can handle it all without our help. So I do not come into agreement with statements like, "Well, God must have needed them in Heaven more than down here." He doesn't need anything. He wants our devotion and love, but He doesn't need anything.

As we left the doctor's office, we were really in some major shock. This was a place we had never been before. All of the other hard and painful experiences we had ever had could not even be compared to this hurt. We slowly walked out to the car. When we sat down in the car, we began to pray. I remember cranking the car up on that overcast day. We prayed, and then we just declared and made up our minds that we would still worship Him. I began to declare that He is good, and we worshipped Him in the car in the parking lot. Then the tears came. We cried a broken cry. I could not control the tears or cries that came out. We were broken, but our hearts were set to worship Him no matter what. I couldn't even pull out of the parking lot of the doctor's office for a while.

Then we slowly and quietly made the long drive home. We had to be back the next day for the DNC procedure. We were in shock the whole night and had to tell Kaiser that we wouldn't be having that baby anymore, but that we would have to wait to see the baby in heaven. That was a very sad night, to say the least. But, praise God, we had so many friends calling and praying for us. We found out later how tragically often that happens to others. We are not the only ones who have been through this, and God would use this for good in the very near future.

We went to the hospital the next day and had the procedure. After that, we took a couple of days off to get our thoughts together. But we were in church the following Sunday, and our church family was most comforting to us. I know God used our worship to minister to others because we did not for one moment that following Sunday get into self-pity, but we worshipped Him from our hearts.

Dell stayed home that Sunday night to rest, which she totally deserved to do, but I went on to church that night. God used me to pray for one of my ministry partners and when I did, He began to open me up to more power and gifting. I ended up praying, singing, and then singing in the Spirit over my friend, and then also interpreted the song.

When I opened my eyes, the Power of God was so strong on him that he was shaking all over and crying his eyes out. I was moved and amazed by the Power of God that night.

INTERPRETATION OF THE SONG IN TONGUES:
Go to that place in worship,
Go to that Holy place,
Go to that place in worship were Jesus stays!

I said,
Go to that place in worship,
Go to that Holy place,
Go to the Holy of Holies where Jesus stays!

I prayed to God after our loss, and I remembered the story of a mighty man of God. He and his wife had a daughter who faced sickness and disease her entire life and, at the age of eighteen, she went home to be with the Lord. I heard him testify that after the loss, he spoke to God and said that since he had lost his daughter, he wanted back what the enemy had stolen, so he asked for souls. He told the Lord that he wanted to keep preaching and that he wanted God to give him more souls for His kingdom.

I thought about that when we suffered this loss. I thought about the fact that the enemy has to give back what he has stolen. So I began to pray and ask God for a greater anointing on my life and to give me souls for the kingdom too!

The very next Friday night at the HOT HOUSE, I began to share the testimony of how our child did not make it, but that we worshiped God through it all. This testimony moved so many, and young people were touched and impacted powerfully by our commitment to God.

The following Tuesday morning, I spoke at the Jeff Davis County Middle School. I spoke at a Fellowship of Christian Athletes (FCA) meeting. There were about thirty students there that morning. This was the first time I had ever spoken in this school. I quickly shared how God had set me free from all the drugs and alcohol. Then I began to share with them about the loss of my child. God began to move on their hearts. I gave an altar call for salvation and rededication. When I did, I asked for those who were ready to commit to raise their hands and let me see them. So many hands went up that I asked them if they would, to come and take a knee with me and let me lead them in a prayer. When I did the entire class, except for one student, got out of their seats and came over and committed their lives to Jesus Christ! There were about thirty of them!

While we were starting to pray, the bell rang for them to go to class. I was just going to pray anyway, but the coach said, "Don't worry about that!"

I replied, "O, I'm not!" We all prayed and then let the kids go to their classes. God was already giving children back to me!

Not many weeks after this loss, God gave me a dream. In the dream my heart was torn again. I can remember seeing a young girl with a head full of beautiful brown hair, but I couldn't make out her face. I wanted to get to her so badly. My heart yearned to get to her, but I couldn't. I also saw a boy that was very tall and I knew I could get to him, he was mine. But I wanted that little girl and I couldn't have her. When I woke up, the Lord began to show what all of it meant. I believe the interpretation is that we were going to have a little girl, but we weren't going to get to have her now. And the boy was to be the one that we would get to have. I believe since he was so big that we will get to see him grow up too.

Then I remembered that God had already shown Ms. Bonnie what we were going to have. So I wanted to ask her and see if I had interpreted my dream correctly. After the loss, she told us that before the baby went to be with the Lord, that what the Lord had shown her, He had changed. Whatever we were going to have was now going to be different from what we would have next.

So I told her my dream. She knows a lot about dreams and interpretation too. After I told it to her, I said, "I believe we were going to have a girl, but now we will have a boy next."

She wouldn't agree or disagree, but simply said that she would pray and see if God wanted her to tell me before she said anything.

It was only a week or so before she gave me the answer.

My dream had been right on and so had the interpretation. My daughter had gone on to be with the Lord, and we believe the next child we will have will be a son. This was comforting and extremely sad, all at the same time. Now I know that we have a daughter. She is already in heaven. How I long for her, though we have never met. I want to be with her terribly bad.

I told my family and tell others that our family is bigger already, but that there is just one wild Jackson running around heaven waiting for us. I also say that we are batting a thousand because Kaiser gave his life to Jesus at age six, and our little girl is already in heaven. Our family is bigger; we will just have to wait to see our daughter.

God receives all the little children, I guarantee. My daughter is not lost, but she is where I want to be, and one day we will all be reunited. She is with Jesus and will never have to face a day of heartache or pain. I often ask Jesus to just let her know that it is hard down here on earth and sometimes daddy doesn't do what he should or act like he should, but to tell her that daddy loves Jesus and is trying to do his best. I don't pray to her because that would be idolatry, but I know Jesus won't mind letting her know how much her mommy, daddy, and brother wanted her and how much we love her. I am confident that we will all be united as a family one day, along with our sweet, precious, and loving Savior, Jesus.

Chapter Thirteen

Do Not Neglect Salvation

Hebrews 2:3, "How shall we escape if we neglect so great a salvation?"

Salvation is the most amazing thing that can take place in a person's life. It is the very moment of Spiritual conception! It is the time when you are born again. We are all born of water, but not all of Spirit. Old Nicodemus heard it straight from the mouth of Jesus.

John 3:3-8, "Then Jesus answered and said to him, 'Most assuredly, I say to you, unless one is born again, he cannot see the kingdom of God.' Nicodemus said to Him, 'How can a man be born when he is old? Can he enter a second time into his mother's womb and be born?' Jesus answered, 'Most assuredly, I say to you, unless one is born of water and the Spirit, he cannot enter the kingdom of God. That which is born of the flesh is flesh, and that which is born of the Spirit is spirit. Do not marvel that I say to you; 'You must be born again.' The wind blows where it wishes, and you hear the sound of it, but cannot tell where it comes from and where it goes. So is everyone who is born of the Spirit.'"

Being saved, or born again, is paramount. We must be born again. It is truly the most amazing blessing from the Lord. He causes our spirit man to come alive. He creates in us new life. He allows us to be in oneness with Him by our spirit coming to life, and then sealing us with the Holy Spirit of promise. He does this to create an avenue of communion that the unsaved cannot have.

The Holy Spirit and our conscience brings conviction

and promptings to let us know the directions we should take in life, but true communion and revelation can only come through a salvation experience where we are born again.

He told Nicodemus that unless we are born again we couldn't even see the kingdom of God. We can only have clear understanding about the things of God by revelation from God, the Holy Spirit. He is the person of the Godhead who teaches us and reveals the scriptures, and the very heart of God, the Father, to us.

So many, after giving their lives to Jesus, seem to forget how great a blessing they have received, so their lives and walk with God begin to grow cold and stagnant. We should never lose our fire and our fervency for Jesus and what He has done for us and wants to do for every person on the planet. We must never neglect so great a salvation!

The scripture from Hebrews says, how shall we escape if we neglect so great a salvation? If our salvation becomes a trivial thing, how shall we escape the curse of sin? We only escape through Jesus. And I just want to encourage every believer to be strong and keep the faith. Don't be skeptical, but be expectant. Don't buy into the lie that is in total opposition to what Jesus said. People say now that you are saved, it is going to be hard, and the devil is going to be after you, and it is going to be so difficult. No, Jesus said in Matthew 11:29, "Come to Me, all you who labor and are heavy laden, and I will give you rest. Take *My* yoke upon you and learn from Me, for I am gentle and lowly in heart, and you will find rest for your souls. For My yoke is easy and My burden is light."

The dinky devil is always coming against us. Life does not get harder with Jesus. The trials of life will always come, but now, through salvation, you have someone to take you through them. He said in His word, "...you will find rest for your souls." I am not saying there will not be any tribulation coming your way. Jesus actually reassures us that there will be tribulation in this world, but tells us to be of good cheer because He, Himself, has overcome the world.

John 16:33, "In the world you will have tribulation; but be of good cheer, I have overcome the world."

Jesus has overcome every obstacle and trial and tribulation that we will ever have to face, and He will face every one of them with us. He is for us, not against us! He is our Love King, we need to lift our hands and receive the ring! Receive the ring of the Love King! We must hold on to our salvation and remember what God has brought us out of. Let us not ever get complacent. Let us not ever come to a meeting or wake up to a day where we are not expecting to encounter Him and His presence. He will never leave us or forsake us. We can trust Jesus. If we don't, we really aren't saved anyway.

To believe actually means to trust in, adhere to, and rely upon. If there is no trust, you do not truly believe. That is what it means to give Lordship to another, to completely turn over ownership and trust. We stop trusting in our own abilities and start trusting and relying on God's ability.

Be encouraged to trust Jesus. There is not one person on this planet, who has given their lives to Jesus and been filled with His Spirit, who wishes that they hadn't done it.

When I used and abused all the drugs and alcohol, I lived by a standard of—I would do a certain drug unless I found one I liked better. When I found something I liked better, I would use it instead of some other drug. The same way with liquor drinks. But I tell you, when I found Jesus, I put down every bit of the weed, the cocaine, the ecstasy, the pills and the liquor, because I found something better than any of it! I actually found some One better than all of it. He is worth throwing anything this world has to offer down for.

He is for us! He is for us! There is no condemnation in Him! Jesus did not come to condemn but to save. He came for you and me. He came "to seek and to save that which was lost." (Luke 19:10). We think we are the ones doing the seeking, but He has actually been seeking for you and me our entire lives. This Love King desperately wants to be with you.

He wants you to experience His one of a kind, genuine, undeserving, unhindered, un-perverted, unfailing, amazing, fulfilling, completing, all-encompassing love.

SONG OF PROPHECY:
No condemnation, no condemnation,
From coast to coast all over this nation!

He does not condemn us for our sin, He forgives us of it when we admit we have it and turn from it. Forgiveness does not take place because we sin, but He is faithful and just and if we confess our sins, He will forgive us. That is why He came to take away the sins of the world.

John 1:29, "The next day John saw Jesus coming toward him, and said, 'Behold! The Lamb of God who takes away the sin of the world!'"

Romans 8:1, "There is therefore now no condemnation to those who are in Christ Jesus, who do not walk according to the flesh, but according to the Sprit."

1 John 1:9, "If we confess our sins, He is faithful and just to forgive us our sins and to cleanse us from all unrighteousness."

The greatest passage of scripture to me that shows His overwhelming love and desire not to condemn, is in the book of John. It is the story of the woman caught in adultery. Let's see the real Jesus and how precious our salvation is.

John 8:3-11, "Then the scribes and Pharisees brought to Him a woman caught in adultery. And when they had set her in the midst, they said to Him, 'Teacher, this woman was caught in adultery, in the very act. Now Moses, in the law, commanded us that such should be stoned. But what do You say?' This they said, testing Him, that they might have something of which to accuse Him. But Jesus stooped down and wrote on the ground with His finger, as though He did not hear. So when they continued asking Him, He raised Himself up and said to them, 'He who is without sin among you, let him throw a stone at her first.' And again He stooped down and wrote on the ground. Then those who heard it, being convicted by their conscience, went out one by one, beginning with the oldest even to the last. And Jesus was left alone, and the woman standing in the midst. When Jesus raised Himself up and saw no one but the woman, He said to her, 'Woman, where are those accusers of yours? Has no one condemned you?' She said, 'No one, Lord.

"And Jesus said to her, 'Neither do I condemn you; go and sin no more.'"

This is the perfect picture of Jesus fulfilling the scriptures, telling of who He was. (John 1:29) The woman who had sinned was doubtlessly guilty. She was caught. The haughty Pharisees even added the phrase, "In the very act." So this is the picture of a person completely guilty and caught in their sin and then coming face-to-face with Jesus Christ. And what did He do? Did He send her straight to hell? Did He put her down and tell her it would take months or years to get close to God again because of this sin? Did He make her feel terrible? No! He wanted the guys who busted her to remember that they too had sin in their lives and to stop judging others. But for the woman who was in bondage to her sin, He showed her in the most loving and compassionate way, that sin is not ok with Him. He showed her that He loved her, but the sin was what He hated. He showed her the greatest love that can be shown, forgiveness and mercy. He is truly compassionate.

He asked, "Has no one condemned you?"

She replied, "No one, Lord." And we then get to see the beautiful heart of our Savior.

"Neither do I condemn you." Hallelujah! He does not condemn! NO CONDEMNATION, NO CONDEMNATION, FROM COAST TO COAST ALL OVER THIS NATION!

John 3:16-17, "For God so loved the world that He gave His only begotten Son, that whoever believes in Him should not perish but have everlasting life. For God did not send His

Son into the world to condemn the world, but that the world through Him might be saved."

Jesus came to save the world. He came so that the world through Him might be saved. He did not come to condemn. If you are in sin today, cry out to Jesus right now; do not wait another second; He wants to set you free. He does not want to condemn you. He wants you to be in relationship with Him. He wants you to draw near to Him and then He will draw near to you.

John 15:16, "You did not choose Me, but I chose you." This awesome God loves you and me enough to go ahead and choose us, while we were still sinners, and pay the debt we owed, for us. This is truly some good news, to say the least.

I beg you today, if you have never accepted Jesus Christ and His forgiveness and love, to do so today. His yoke is easy and His burden is light. He has overcome the world. And He longs to be with you in the most intimate relationship and fellowship. He is the friend who sticks closer than a brother. He will never leave you. Even if your family forsakes you, or has already, He said He wouldn't!

Isaiah 49:15-16, "Can a woman forget her nursing child, and not have compassion on the son of her womb? Surely they may forget, yet I will not forget you. See, I have inscribed you on the palms of My hands."

Jesus inscribed you on the palms of His hands when He took the nails that held Him on the cross. He can never forget you. You are forever inscribed in Him and His thoughts are on you.

If you have, at one time in your life, surrendered to the call of the Master, but today you can check your life and it is not as fruitful as it should be, I encourage you to rededicate it to Him whole-heartedly. A life surrendered to God is a powerful thing. And your level of commitment to God can and will affect everyone around you.

Romans 8:38-39, "For I am persuaded that neither death

nor life, nor angels nor principalities nor powers, nor things present nor things to come, nor height nor depth, nor any other created thing, shall be able to separate us from the love of God which is in Christ Jesus our Lord."

Romans 5:6-10, "For when we were still without strength, in due time Christ died for the ungodly. For scarcely for a righteous man will one die; yet perhaps for a good man someone would even dare to die. But God demonstrates His own love toward us, in that while we were still sinners, Christ died for us. Much more then, having now been justified by His blood, we shall be saved from wrath through Him. For if when we were enemies we were reconciled to God through the death of His Son, much more, having been reconciled, we shall be saved by His life."

2 Corinthians 5:17-21, "Therefore, if anyone is in Christ, he is a new creation; old things have passed away; behold, all things have become new. Now all things are of God, who has reconciled us to Himself through Jesus Christ, and has given us the ministry of reconciliation, that is, that God was in Christ reconciling the world to Himself, not imputing their trespasses to them, and has committed to us the word of reconciliation. Now then, we are ambassadors for Christ, as though God were pleading through us: we implore you on Christ's behalf, be reconciled to God. For He made Him who knew no sin to be sin for us, that we might become the righteousness of God in Him."

I hope you can see that Jesus is for you and not against you. Salvation is your beginning. I pray you step into this relationship with Jesus, and if you have already, I hope you are stirred to begin to walk in the Spirit and power of God and to step out of the boat of doubt and unbelief and walk on the water of the supernatural. The Kingdom of God is yours, please take it and continue to write the book of Acts. You get to pick up where that book left off and write the next chapters with your life.

Romans 3:23, "...for all have sinned and fall short of the

glory of God."

Romans 6:23, "For the wages of sin is death, but the gift of God is eternal life in Christ Jesus our Lord."

Romans 10:9-10, "...that if you confess with your mouth the Lord Jesus and believe in your heart that God has raised Him from the dead, you will be saved. For with the heart one believes unto righteousness, and with the mouth confession is made unto salvation."

Romans 10:13, "For whoever calls on the name of the LORD shall be saved."

So you can pray this prayer or any prayer from your heart, and with your mouth, and you shall be saved. Just cry out to God with your whole heart and God will save you. Just believe and receive salvation by faith, and then press on to live holy and for Jesus all the rest of your days.

SALVATION PRAYER:

Dear Jesus, I confess, I have sinned and fallen short, but right now, Father, in the name of Jesus, I ask you to forgive me of my sins and to wash me clean in the blood of Jesus. I accept the price He paid for me on the cross. I give you my life and I ask you to take it and make something great out of it. Jesus, I confess that you came in the flesh and that you died on the cross, and that you rose again, and that you are alive forevermore. I give you my life. I confess you are my LORD and my Savior. I am yours and You are mine.

Thank You for paying the price for my sin and accepting me, and not condemning me.

PRAYER FOR BAPTISM WITH THE HOLY SPIRIT:

Father, I ask You, in the name of Jesus, to baptize and fill me with Your Holy Spirit. I want to receive power from on high. If Your first disciples needed this filling, and Jesus You told them to wait for it, I need it and I am waiting for it now. I thank You that I am receiving this filling and empowerment now. You promised it to me and I want it now. Fill me from head to toe in, Jesus' name. I receive this fresh baptism in Jesus' name. Thank you Father!

Tom Jackson
May 2010

For booking or to order more books:

FlameThrower Ministries, Inc.
760 Oak Grove Church Road
Rhine, Georgia 31077

www.facebook.com/hothousemcrae

Tom Jackson's email:

tkaiserj27@yahoo.com

www.ingramcontent.com/pod-product-compliance
Lightning Source LLC
Chambersburg PA
CBHW071127090426
42736CB00012B/2043